FULL LIVES

Women Who Have Freed Themselves
from Food & Weight Obsession

Lindsey Hall

gürze books

Full Lives:
Women Who Have Freed Themselves from Food & Weight Obsession

©1993 by Lindsey Hall

Gürze Books
P.O. Box 2238
Carlsbad, CA 92018
(619) 434-7533

Cover and book design by Abacus Graphics, Oceanside, CA

"Dessert" ©1993 by Geneen Roth

A portion of author royalties from this book will be donated to non-profit eating disorders associations.

Library of Congress
Cataloging-in-Publication Data

Full lives : women who have freed themselves from food & weight obsession / by Lindsey Hall.
   p. cm.
   ISBN 0-936077-26-3 (pbk.) : $12.95
   1. Eating disorders. 2. Women--Mental health. 3. Eating disorders--Patients--United States--Biography. I. Hall, Lindsey, 1949-
RC552.E18F85   1992   92-36287
616.85'26'0082--dc20   CIP

NOTE:
The authors and publisher of this book intend for this publication to provide accurate information. It is sold with the understanding that it is meant to complement, not substitute for, professional medical and/or psychological services.

First Edition

2 4 6 8 0 9 7 5 3 1

Table of Contents

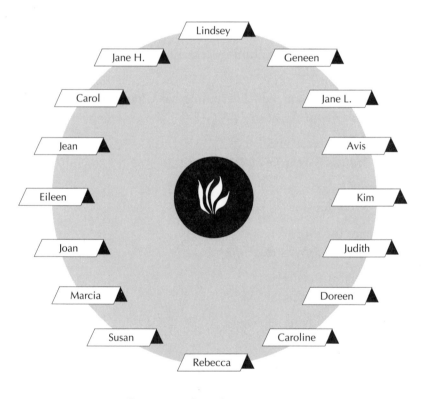

Seating Arrangement

The Invitation

You are invited to a dinner party with sixteen extraordinary women who have freed themselves from obsessions with food and weight. You may already know many of them, because included are bestselling authors, highly respected clinicians, speakers, and directors of national associations—all dedicated to the prevention of eating disorders and the end of society's preoccupation with thinness. What you may not know is that every one of them has experienced thinness madness and the subsequent struggle to be free. They know first-hand that a life consumed by an obsession with food and weight is an empty one and, more importantly, they are proof that radical, personal transformation is entirely possible.

*I was introduced to the idea of a spiritual banquet by Kim Chernin at the end of her book, **The Obsession**, in reference to artist Judy Chicago's exhibit, "The Dinner Party." There, Chernin describes an assembly of women of "symbolic meaning and accomplishment," celebrating their own and each other's "rediscovered power and joy" over a meal together. She goes on to wish that Alma, an anorexic, female soul, join this party not only to partake of the feast and celebration, but also to be nourished by the kinship and richness of the guests.*

The **Full Lives** dinner party to which you are invited is just such a celebration. The authors who are gathered here are women of actual "meaning and accomplishment." They have overcome body shame, compulsive eating, anorexia nervosa, bulimia, yo-yo dieting, and other debilitating problems with food, and have devoted their professional lives to helping others do the same. When asked to collaborate in this feast of ideas, which could support those still struggling with these issues, every one of them enthusiastically agreed.

I, too, fit the criteria to be considered a member of this group. I struggled with bulimia for nine years, successfully recovered, and have actively contributed to the eating disorders field for well over a decade. In 1980, my husband, Leigh Cohn, and I told my story in a booklet titled, "Eat Without Fear," the first publication ever written solely about bulimia. Committed to increasing public awareness about this disorder, I began speaking to college audiences throughout the United States, was a guest on dozens of radio shows, and was the first bulimic to appear on national television. Leigh and I wrote two more booklets as more information about eating disorders came to light, including the experiences of other individuals recovering from problems with food.

In 1986, we combined the booklets into a book titled, **BULIMIA: A Guide to Recovery** and later went on to write and publish additional books, including **Self-Esteem Tools for Recovery**. We also created "The Gürze Eating Disorders Bookshelf Catalogue," a comprehensive, mail-order resource for books and tapes on food problems of all kinds. Publishing this catalogue, as well as several of the books in it, has placed practically every new book on these and related topics in our hands. It has also brought us in touch with authors, therapists, families, and many others concerned with food and weight issues.

The idea for a collaboration came to me during a relaxing hot bath several years ago. I was feeling particularly thankful for the life I was then leading, when I realized that none of it would have happened had I not recovered from bulimia. Healing my abusive relationship with food forced me to look at every fear, every pain, every barrier that I had erected to keep myself from living and loving fully. What's more, the very act of eating had become something positive—an affirmation of my self-worth and growth as a person.

Stunned by the thought that I actually had my eating disorder to thank for my "rediscovered power and joy," I wondered how many other people felt this same way. I began to contact other women whom I knew had both overcome these kinds of problems and were actively working in the field. All had a similar response—healing their unhealthy relationships with food caused many positive, far-reaching changes in their lives—and they were eager to join together in an anthology.

As the number of women who wanted to contribute grew, so did my excitement. I knew that a chorus of voices would be powerful inspiration for healing both on a personal and cultural level. So, using a book as a vehicle, I arranged for us all to "meet" at this dinner party, symbolic of our unity and freedom around food. I encouraged the authors to "speak" on whatever aspect of recovery they felt most strongly contributed to the fullness of their present lives, and asked them to tell their own stories in the process.

Each one also agreed to contribute a portion of their royalty payments to various non-profit associations dedicated to eating disorders education and prevention.

One interesting aspect of the editing process was deciding how to structure the chapters (or arrange the seating, if you will), but after having worked on this book with these extraordinary women for almost three years, it turned out to be easy. Some have been friends for years, others have similarities either in their personal or professional lives. As hostess, I will introduce each author and her chapter, with a little bit about who they are, how I know them, and their chapter topics.

This book was written for the growing number of individuals, particularly women, who are discovering that the relentless cultural emphasis on their appearance both denies and devalues the more personally meaningful aspects of their lives. Although plagued with symptoms which revolve around food, they are deeply, profoundly hungry for something else.

This hunger is experienced in many ways and at different levels, as the chapters which follow will show. More often than not, it is mistaken for physical hunger, and as such, is kept under strict control via dieting, purging, or constant scrutiny. However, even individuals who binge-eat and lose control around food continue to feel hungry long after experiencing the physical sensation of fullness. This is because the empty place is not about food—it is about nourishment, not just for the body but for the soul.

The issues surrounding nourishment hold particular meaning for women whose role has traditionally been to "feed" and see to the needs of others before taking care of themselves. Although roles are certainly changing for both sexes, women have continued to place less importance on their needs and dreams, reflecting society's emphasis on the success and fulfillment of men. What's more, the meaning of success and fulfillment has been largely defined by and for men, without taking into account women's unique perspectives. Viewed within this context, giving one's self permission to eat and grow large as a woman, complete with female urges, instincts, motivations, and powers, then becomes an act of social and political significance—a big step for anyone to take.

This book, therefore, is not about "how to" overcome your problems with food, but rather "why to." Why give up something that provides even temporary feelings of protection, companionship, numbness, fullness, self-esteem, and success? Why go through what might be years of self-inquiry, challenging cultural norms and parental values, seeking one's own inner truth, and even questioning the meaning of life, only to have to live in a world that has done none of that work?

The answers lie in the lives and stories of the women in this book.

Now, with great love and respect, I welcome you to join us for dinner! May you be nourished by the wisdom, courage, and kinship of these extraordinary women, and may you be inspired to lead a full life of your own.

Jane Hirschmann & Carol Munter

At the **Full Lives** dinner table, Jane R. Hirschmann and Carol Munter are seated to my immediate right. Actually, the conversation in the chapter which follows did take place at an Italian restaurant in downtown San Diego, when they were near my home to give one of their "Overcoming Overeating" weekend workshops. We had prearranged to tape the evening's discussion as the basis for their chapter to be titled, "My Dinner with Jane and Carol." We had never met, but it didn't take long for us to be deeply engaged in this honest, informative, and mutually enjoyable discussion.

Jane and Carol, who are both New York psychotherapists, are also the co-authors of the book **Overcoming Overeating**, an international bestseller based on an anti-dieting philosophy. Their advice is to feed on demand, "legalize" all foods so that nothing is "forbidden," and learn to separate as well as satisfy physical and emotional hungers without being compulsive. They travel extensively, giving workshops and lectures to thousands of people who are finding success with this approach. Their work has been featured in numerous magazines and newspapers; and, as the debate about the effectiveness of dieting rages on, they continue to frequently appear on television and radio shows. My catalogue has carried their book and workshop tapes, and Gürze Books recently published a re-release of Jane's *first book, **Preventing Childhood Eating Problems**, which she wrote with Lela Zaphiropoulos.*

During our dinner conversation that night, I was amazed at Jane and Carol's combined vitality, intelligence, dedication, and willingness to share ideas. I was particularly impressed by the way in which they worked together as a team. They listened to each other, supported and challenged ideas, laughed, questioned, and even kicked each other under the table in their excitement. All in all, they appeared to be nourished by their friendship, a metaphor which has stuck with me to this day.

Whether by biological design or social conditioning, women like to feel a sense of connection. However, by overvaluing autonomy, competition, and individuation, our society has undermined one of the basic motivating factors in their lives—being in empathic, mutually-empowering relationships. The quest for thinness has not brought women together, it has separated us; and, in the failure to measure up, left us with feelings of inadequacy and loneliness.

*The authors of **Full Lives** have spent years caught in this quest and the subsequent struggle to become free. We know the difference between the fantasy of a full life and the real thing. We also know the rewards of personal transformation, and that the support of other women is invaluable. Jane and Carol's collaboration is but one example of the strength and joy that blossoms when women unite; and so, we invite you to join us at this dinner that we might feast upon each other's stories of the past and visions for the future.*

My Dinner with Jane & Carol

Jane R. Hirschmann & Carol Munter

LINDSEY: When did you two meet?

JANE: We met in New York in 1978. Carol had been running anti-diet groups since 1970, and I was a psychotherapist at a mental health center. I had already been introduced to the anti-dieting philosophy and had used it to resolve my own eating problem. I wanted to meet "the guru," so I called her to ask if I could watch her work. My intent was to help other women with their food problems. Carol invited me to observe her Thursday night group, which I did. I remember sitting next to her, but a little off from the others...

CAROL: It was funny—there was this silent person sitting at my side.

JANE: But the group got used to me. I stayed for a long time—I think twelve weeks. I sat and watched. Although I was doing similar work when I came to Carol, it was the best education I could get. I bodies because the other message is so pervasive.

LINDSEY: It's brainwashing of its own!

JANE: Right. My children have been brought up to believe that dieting is dangerous. My twelve-year-old twins sometimes come home very upset saying so-and-so is "taking" a diet. They don't call it "going" on a diet. This is their own language. Dieting is like taking dreadful medicine. They see it as self-punishing, and are very upset with their friends who are already in that diet mode.

I have told my kids, who happen to be into sports, that if ever they try to regulate their weight to fit into what they're doing, they get pulled out immediately. And I tell parents—whether their children are dancers, gymnasts, cheerleaders, swimmers, weight lifters, or whatever—to pull them out if there is weight regulation.

I'm starting to talk to them about weight gain now because they're pre-teen. Nobody prepares teenage girls for the fact that they're *supposed* to gain weight! When it comes on it's seen as fat. Actually, on average, they're supposed to gain ten pounds a year during adolescence until they reach maturity. This is a shocking number! Children don't understand. They start out as little human beings and triple their birth weight in the first year of life. The next greatest growth spurt is in adolescence and nobody prepares them for it. For girls, the weight gain is in the hips and the breasts in preparation for child bearing. Even though this is a natural process, they're in shock, their parents are in shock, and everybody is very worried about it all.

LINDSEY: Do you think that more women are getting sick of diets and body hatred?

JANE: Yes. There is a movement afoot. And, that's one reason that our book, *Overcoming Overeating,* is now in its seventh printing, and we're being asked to do more workshops and talks around the country. There is greater interest. When we started this work people thought we were just crazy. But now, with all the scientific evidence that has come out proving how dangerous and ineffective dieting is, some people are looking at alternative ideas. But there's still a pull to get back into dieting...

CAROL: You see, people don't trust themselves. They cannot imagine that you actually do self-regulate when you don't have very rigid rules.

JANE: In the workshop this morning, I asked the group to think about other areas in their lives where they had lifted restrictions. People talked about college when they made the dorms co-ed and had no curfews. There wasn't wanton sex. The young men became your friends, you did your school work, you went to bed early, and not everybody was screwing in the halls. But people think that without restrictions like diets and other food plans, they will go wild, be insatiable and out of control, when actually the reverse happens—they gain control.

LINDSEY: How do you convince someone that their life will be better when they give up the dieting and the restrictions?

CAROL: One of the best benefits is that they will begin to discover what the real issues are that are troubling them. The question, "Why should I give up dieting or food compulsion?" really translates to, "Do I want to spend my life thinking that I have an eating or weight problem, and trying to solve that problem, when in fact that's not the problem at all. Of course, facing and working on the real issues in life fuels people's resistance. Even though it's painful to live within the confines of an eating and weight obsession, it's familiar. It offers a certain kind of hope that if you lose weight your life will be better. Without the weight obsession, you're going to face a lot of things that obviously you've been very afraid to look at.

JANE: Also, what we hear over and over, and what we experience in our own lives, is that when you start addressing the when, the what, and the how much of eating, you're really addressing who you are, what life means to you, and how you want to be in this world. When women allow themselves the food they need when they are hungry, they begin to see that there are other things that they hunger for as well. They may not change an ounce of their body size, but they transform their lives by ending this addiction and finding their own voices. Their lives are totally changed. They are empowered.

I'll give you two short examples. Many years ago, I belonged to a liberal mental health organization and people there wanted to know more about the work I was doing. I organized a panel which included several women from my eating groups. At one point, a female psychiatrist in the audience said, "Okay, I've heard how you've broken your addiction to food, but I want to know what it has meant in your life besides that."

The panel all thought for a few moments and then the first woman said, "I'm a woman who works in the auto industry on the assembly line and I've taken a lot of flak from men because there are not many women who are out there. Has this approach changed my life? Well, I joined NOW and I'm the political action coordinator. It just happened naturally, the process of feeling more empowered."

The second person said, "I think that because of this process, I was able to come out. I'm a lesbian. I was very closeted and after this process I decided that I needed to tell my parents and my community who I was. I really had to be seen for who I was."

CAROL: A lot of people feel enormously relieved that they can really break what feels to them like an addiction to food. I don't think that when people first come to us they even imagine that it would be possible to get to a point where it didn't occur to them to eat unless they were hungry. That seems an absolutely unimaginable goal. Our experience bears out that it is absolutely within the reach of anybody who is willing to really say "no more" to dieting. What then happens with people's lives? They discover that resolving their problem with food is a first step in really getting to work on what will bring vitality and meaning to their lives.

JANE: I would like to add to that that we don't think that you cure the problem and you immediately get love and joy in your life. I think that you cure the problem and then you get yourself back, whoever you are. What you do then is really up to you. Life is very, very complicated. People are very complicated. But without the food compulsions, they at least have a chance to discover what it is that makes them tick and where they want to make interventions and where they don't.

CAROL: You know people spend a lot of time going to therapists and counselors saying, "Please help me with my eating problem. Please help me with my weight problem." But when people stop dieting and put themselves on demand feeding and go to a therapist, they'll say, "I have a problem with anger," or "I have a problem with envy," or "I'm very depressed a lot of the time." And they are actually going to be able to work on that issue. We teach people to eat their way to mental health.

JANE: I think the reason that we can still get turned on about these workshops after all these years is that we know that when we stand up in front of an audience, a large percentage of that audience is going to do what we suggest and they are going to live radically different lives as a result. This is a tremendous turn-on. But the radically different life that we're talking about is a non-addicted life, not necessarily a non-problematic life. We can't promise that.

CAROL: We like to turn people into good investigators. We enlist people's curiosity. We think it's curious that anybody would reach for food when she wasn't physiologically hungry. And we hope to interest people in that event. We want them to become very good explorers of themselves.

JANE: We do weekly workshops in New York for people who've read our book and are working with our approach. These workshops are so exciting because we meet women who are really involved in revolutionary activity. It's so impressive. They really struggle with the issues.

CAROL: In these workshops everybody is working very hard on coming up with solutions, knowing that none of us has all the answers, but we all respect and support each other in our journeys. I remember last summer's bathing suit discussion, which was fabulous. People of all sizes were in the room discussing how we all hated the fact that summer was here. We had to get new bathing suits, and we started talking about it. The group came up with this notion that it's amazing that three quarters of the year living in New York City you have to be fully clothed wherever you go—in front of your neighbors, your children, your colleagues, your in-laws, your friends. Suddenly, two months of the year, you're supposed to strip naked and prance around feeling totally comfortable strutting and showing it all! How come we are all supposed to feel wonderful about this? No wonder we're all terrified. But most people thought they were terrified of getting into the suit because they weren't the right size. Everyone realized that there's a lot more to walking around in a bathing suit than the size you happen to be that year.

LINDSEY: Obviously giving up dieting and food compulsions takes courage. How do you motivate people to let go of such a big part of their lives?

CAROL: I always say to them, "Do you have anything better to do?"

Jean Rubel

Seated next to Jane and Carol is another pioneer, Jean Rubel. I first met Jean in 1980 through her newsletter, the "ANRED Alert," a copy of which was given to me by a friend. Written in a personal, straight-forward style, it answered questions and gave encouragement to readers struggling with food issues. Miraculously, it was being published only a hundred miles or so from my home. I sent the editor a copy of the booklet I had written about my struggle with bulimia, and we soon spoke on the phone. At the earliest convenient time, I drove to Grover City, a small California costal town, where Jean lived and maintained the ANRED office.

Not knowing what to expect, I found a relaxed, level-headed person, with a twinkle in her eye, who offered me tea and cookies and calmly talked about her goals for ANRED (Anorexia Nervosa & Related Eating Disorders, Inc.), the non-profit association she founded in 1977. She knew what she wanted to accomplish in her work, and has remained true to this mission in the dozen-plus years that I've known her. To this day, ANRED continues to be a valuable source of information, and Jean, who is President, still writes the monthly newsletter. Although she moved to Eugene, Oregon several years ago, we have stayed in touch. She loves to talk on the phone.

of her own, and the two of us adopted an us-against-the-world attitude. Together we nursed fantasies of becoming women like the characters played by Lauren Bacall in movies with Humphrey Bogart—strong, powerful, competent, sassy, admired, and fascinating. The distance between our fact and Bacall's fantasy was far indeed.

Under my loneliness simmered a lake of molten rage. Sometimes I turned it loose when I felt ignored, criticized, misunderstood, or unloved. Most of the time, though, I held it in the pit of my stomach, where it became the only defense I could find against my belief that I was different—flawed in some critical way that kept me from joining the human race. Unfortunately, I too often turned this hateful energy against myself in storms of self-criticism and loathing.

I began to blame my body for all my problems. If I weren't so ugly, so big, so soft and flabby, I would be happy and popular. I was convinced that a cute, tiny body would fix everything. I was six feet tall and 145 pounds. According to yearbook pictures I was slender and reasonably attractive, but I couldn't see it. More than anything I wanted to be witty, wise, sophisticated, exciting, sexy, beautiful, and *special*. I wanted to be thin, admired, and loved. Instead I felt awkward, shy, fat, defective, and extremely lonely.

At twenty-three, I decided to take charge and remake myself. I would wipe out all feelings of inadequacy and loneliness with one bold stroke: I would be thin. With the dedication of a postulant taking holy vows, I committed myself to a weight-loss program.

My reasoning was pathetically simplistic: I can fix all the things that are wrong in my life by losing weight. When I'm thin, I'll feel good about myself. I will be proud and self-confident, not shy and awkward. I'll be bubbly and outgoing. I'll like myself and so will other people. I'll be poised and confident, able to handle even the biggest problems with a snappy, sophisticated remark. When I'm thin, I'll be someone really special. Other people will welcome me and want me around. I will be very happy.

That kind of foolish logic led to a twelve-year trap named anorexia nervosa and bulimia. I got thin all right, so thin I almost died, but instead of building a happy life, I ruined my health and created more than a decade of depression and misery. Weight loss, my wonderful solution to all my problems, didn't work.

It took me a long time to admit that being thin was never going to make me happy. It took even longer to figure out what would work instead. Now, staring my fiftieth birthday in the face, I have dependable tools I can use to build happiness, self-confidence, and a satisfying life. What's more, I wouldn't trade those tools for the firmest, slimmest, most toned body that ever fit into size 3 designer jeans. I'm not exactly a decrepit pile of sagging flesh, but gravity is beginning to win. In spite of the wrinkles and gray hair though, I'm happier and more satisfied than ever before. I expect things will only get better. The best is yet to come.

Not to say that I don't have my share of problems and frustrations. I certainly do. Now, though, I know how to handle them. Being thin never solved anything. I need better weapons than weight loss to fight life's battles.

thinness, my self-esteem had never been lower. I felt empty, lost, and worthless.

One night, while I was waiting for the casserole I was going to binge on to cook, I tried to imagine what my life would be like if I were normal—whatever that was. I didn't know anymore. What would I do from 5:00 PM, when I got off work, till 10:30 PM, when I went to bed if I didn't grocery shop, cook, stuff myself, vomit, and clean up? I couldn't think of one single thing. As out of touch as I was at that point, I knew I was in trouble. I also realized that if I were going to give up anorexia and bulimia, I must replace them with other things that were at least as compelling as weight management.

Two children running by and yelling for their mother snapped me out of my reverie. I glanced at my watch and saw that it was time to meet Shelly. As I finished the last sip of coffee and walked around the corner to toss the paper cup in a trash barrel, I collided with a young woman who, in spite of the controlled temperature of the covered mall, wore layers of shapeless sweat clothes. She carried a tray heaped with fast food items. As I reached out to steady us both, I noticed two burgers, three burritos, a plate-sized cinnamon roll, two milkshakes, and a handful of candy bars. When I touched her sleeve, I felt an arm no bigger around than a broomstick.

I apologized for not watching where I was going. Her eyes widened with shock, and then narrowed sullenly when she saw that I was looking at her tray. Even though I had not asked for—and certainly didn't deserve—an explanation, she told me with great urgency that she was meeting friends, that she had collected all their orders, that not all this food was hers. Her body language was eloquent—get away and leave me alone. I wanted to say something, to tell her about the lessons I've learned, but she was too defensive. Years ago, in a similar situation when I was confronted by a well-meaning acquaintance, I made some feeble excuse for my pitiful condition and then avoided her for six years. So, not wanting to make an awkward situation worse, I merely smiled and said, "I'm sorry," one more time and left.

Glancing ahead, I saw Shelly coming towards me with that peculiar hopping bounce she has when she's excited. "I found the most excellent dress in Bon Temps! Wait till you see. It'll knock your socks off! Now let's go find shoes."

"Ok," I replied, less than enthusiastic, but not wanting to sit alone anymore. We found the Shoe Box, where Shelly promptly engaged the clerk in a discussion of the proper footwear for her new outfit. It sounded like we would be there awhile. Determined to be a good sport, I sat quietly, and returned to my thoughts about what I needed to recover. Where was I?

Oh, yes. I needed to admit that even though starving and stuffing allowed me to escape my problems temporarily, and feel in control for brief periods of time, they really didn't help me build a satisfying life. I also needed, if I was going to give up anorexia and bulimia, to find other things to put in their place.

The first part was easier than the second. After twelve years of misery, I could finally admit—if only to myself— that being thin meant absolutely nothing in the grand scheme of things. I had been thin, thinner than most people ever dream of being, and what had it gotten me? Not much. Rotten teeth, cold hands and feet, and embarrassing questions from curious people. Its greatest benefit, the belief that I could solve all my problems by making my body little, had turned out to be nothing more than a lie.

The second part was harder. The first replacement for disordered eating that I tried was marriage. I had managed to meet a man on whom I thought the sun rose and set. The day he asked me to marry him I thought I would burst with joy. Somehow this wonderful man was in love with flawed, defective me. I could hardly believe it.

I felt secure enough in that marriage to relax some of my iron-clad control and experiment with new ways of doing things. I learned that I could endure anxiety about weight gain without collapsing. I learned I could push past that anxiety and eat normal meals in spite of my food fears. I learned I could eat three healthy meals a day and not balloon to 500 pounds. I learned that I could work alongside my husband and contribute something important to the business we started together. I learned to feel comfortable in groups of people that I didn't know very well. I learned to trust. I learned to relax and play, to enjoy life without always spoiling things by expecting the worst to happen. Although I learned these lessons slowly, over many months, I did learn them.

And when I also learned that this wonderful man, the man with whom I wanted to spend the rest of my life, had been having affairs all during our marriage, I thought I would die of shame and humiliation. Feeling hurt and angry, I told him to leave. The day he moved out, I sat at the dining room table, by myself, eating a lonely dinner. I drummed my fingernails on the polished surface and toyed with the possibility of returning to my eating disorder. I hadn't starved or stuffed in years, but suddenly the idea was attractive again. After all, I told myself, food and diet books were my good friends for many years. Why not see if they still offer any comfort?

No! My hand slammed on the table. I had managed to be normal for a long time. I wasn't going to toss it all away just because I was hurt and disappointed. I had tasted what real life was all about, and I liked it—the fun and challenge, the aliveness. Returning to disordered eating would be like going back into a padded cell after living free for a while. I got through the divorce and the next year with only two minor lapses.

The next replacement for disordered eating was graduate school. I wanted a career. I wanted to do something I could be proud of. I wanted to matter, to make a difference, to somehow make the world a better place. If I was going to do all that, I needed preparation.

In graduate school I learned to think, to analyze, and to integrate conflicting ideas into a larger perspective. I learned that I always have a choice. I can't control everything that happens to me, but I most certainly *can* control what I do and think about it. I learned that I can choose between different ways of solving problems, either temporarily escaping them through food or alcohol, thereby creating more problems for myself, or dealing with them head on in ways that do not cause more pain. Most important of all, I learned that I am responsible for the kind of life I have. I can't change other people, or child-hood experiences, but I *can* make choices and do things for myself that meet my needs and bring me happiness. I can choose to be a victim or a victor.

"Well, what do you think about this pair?" Startled by Shelly's question, I jumped and knocked the heavy King book off my lap and onto her foot. "Ooh!" she said, "a simple 'No' would have been enough!"

The shoes were cute, and I told her so. After comparing them with others, she decided to take them. "How about some pizza at Little Italy?" she added, referring to one of the fast-food restaurants on the main promenade. "Sounds good," I replied.

When we got there, Shelly ordered a slice of pep-peroni pizza, and I asked for a combo with anchovies. Ignoring her wrinkled nose, I told her I was going back to Coffee Café for another cup of cocoa mocha. I turned the corner and for the second time that day collided with the emaciated young woman in baggy sweat clothes. Still alone, she was wolfing down a double-dip ice cream cone. I saw a box of chocolate mints in her jacket pocket. Recognizing me, her face turned a dull red. Jerking the ice cream cone away, as if to hide it, she set her jaw in stubborn determination. She walked right by me, looking straight ahead. "I'm sorry again," I said. She did not acknowledge the apology. I watched her continue across the tile floor and disappear into the restroom.

I argued with myself. Part of me wanted to follow her, to say something comforting and helpful. The other, more experienced part, knew it would be futile. She would be embarrassed. She would deny she had a problem. She

44

might lie if I pushed too hard, saying she was sick with a stomach flu. If I learned anything from my anorexia and bulimia, it was that recovery has to be done by the person with the disorder. Parents can't do it. Friends can't do it. Neither can spouses or professional counselors. These people can offer support, information, and opportunities for new choices, but when it comes right down to it, behavior changes have to be made by the person herself.

Feeling a little sad, I got my cup of coffee and returned to Shelly. She had taken her new shoes out of their bag and was regarding them with a wrinkled forehead. "Uh-oh," I said to myself. "This doesn't look good. She's got that I-don't-like-these-and-I-want-to-exchange-them look on her face." I found out I was right. Apparently the pizza had revived her, and she bounced off down the promenade with the same energy she had that morning.

I settled into my chair again and glanced around. A poster in the window of a lingerie boutique caught my eye. "Take Control!" advised the ad for girdles. The picture showed a woman shoehorned into a bust-to-thigh rubber and elastic contraption that looked like something out of a medieval torture chamber.

I grinned. That's what I did, I thought. I took control—not of my body, but of my life. I finally learned how to take charge and take care of myself—how to give myself what I need without hurting myself like I did with the eating disorder.

Like everyone else, I need basic things like food, clothes, a place to live, and transportation. To get them I need money. I've learned how to make enough money to buy the things I need as well as many of the things I want.

release blocked energy and recharge my batteries by skiing, hiking, gardening, reading, or goofing off with friends. If I don't play and have fun, I get much too intense and serious. Play is just as necessary for my well-being as food, water, and air.

Swallowing the last of the coffee, I wrapped up my mid-century musing by remembering a recent conversation with a friend I hadn't seen for over twenty years. After hearing about my current work, she asked me if I'm ever afraid I'll slip back into an eating disorder. "Absolutely not!" I told her. I used to diet and binge to comfort and protect myself, to assert my independence, to give myself an illusion of power and control, to give myself an excuse for not growing up and being responsible, to release tension and anxiety, and even to indulge myself. Now I know how to do all these things directly, healthfully, and much more effectively.

What's more, if I wanted my eating disorder back, I'd have to give up something. What would that be? Time spent with friends? Never. ANRED? Don't be ridiculous! Time spent playing with the computer, or gardening or hiking or reading? No. I love these things. Trading any of them for an eating disorder would leave me in emotional poverty. Now that I've learned how to take charge of my life and get what I need, why would I return to something as empty as starving or stuffing? That doesn't make any sense at all.

Feeling restored by the snack and time out, I gathered myself together and set off to find Shelly. She was in the Shoe Box paying for two more pairs of shoes. "Wait till you see them. They're knock-outs!" she enthused. "I couldn't decide which pair to wear to my party so I got them all."

"What's the big deal about this party?" I asked.

"You blockhead," she teased. "Haven't you guessed? It's for your birthday. I wanted to keep it a surprise, but I'm busting to tell you. I wanted to look special for your Big Five-O."

"Umm," I replied, breaking out my biggest grin. "Then let's go back to those t-shirts. There's one I want to wear to the party."

"What?" screeched Shelly. "I've just spent all this time and money for a gorgeous outfit, and you're going to wear a t-shirt? Please don't tell me it's that flamingo-pink one," she added, looking horrified.

"No, not that one. The blue one with the beads and sequins. The one that says, 'Don't you wish you're this good when you're 50?'"

Eileen T. Bills

*S*everal times in my life there have appeared individuals to whom I am instantly and mysteriously devoted. Eileen T. Bills is one of those people. Initially, she wrote to thank me for the inspiration she received from a booklet I had written in 1980. I was so moved by her words that I reprinted part of her original, hand-written, three-page letter in my book, **BULIMIA: A Guide to Recovery**, when it was published six years later. Shortly afterward came another note from Eileen, who said she had seen the new book and was surprised and happy to see her letter in it. We continued corresponding and spoke on the phone from time to time. She has also been in touch with Jean Rubel all these years, so I thought it appropriate to seat them together at the **Full Lives** dinner party.

I learned about Eileen's interest in the topic of sexual abuse when she sent me a copy of her dissertation, "Eating Disorders and Their Correlates in Earlier Episodes of Incest," which led me to ask her about writing a chapter for this book. Although she had never attempted to write about her own experiences, nor was I aware of the full extent of the abuse she had endured, I sensed that there would be power and inspiration in her story.

When I got her initial draft, I noticed a curious thing. After the first few pages of introduction, the narrative slipped from the first to the third person as she began describing specific incidents of sexual abuse in more detail. Apparently, it was

From Sexual Abuse to Empowerment

Eileen T. Bills

"I therefore put forward the thesis that at the bottom of every case of hysteria there are one or more occurrences of premature sexual experiences, occurrences which belong in the earliest years of childhood" (Freud, 1905). At that time, anorexia nervosa was considered a hysterical neurosis (Lasegue, 1873; Janet, 1903).

The Travesty

My mother was very unhappy when I was a little girl. She cried all the time and fought wretchedly with my father. Sometimes the fighting got so bad that the neighbors called the police.

My father was usually a passive participant in these fights. While my mother was screaming hysterically, he would just walk away. This would upset my mother even more and she would go after him. Finally, his control would give way and he would spew out some vicious remark and shove my mother back. Eventually, one or the other would decide that it was time to get away. Frequently, my father would make motions to leave but my mother would get in the car and take off first. Then there was a struggle as to who would take the car. My mom usually won and would not return for days. I remember one time my father getting into the car, but my mother would not let him leave her and got in too. They drove away and left me alone. The next morning my father had stitches in his head, the car was smashed, and he showed me his blood drenched shirt saying, "See what your mother did to me!"

I was very afraid when they fought, but stayed close, believing that my presence prevented them from hurting each other too badly. Most of the time, they didn't even notice me pleading with them to stop, nor were they careful about what they said or did in front of me. Going to sleep at night was awful when my parents were fighting. Our house felt empty and cold, and I felt alone and unsafe.

My father owned and operated a motel on the beach, and our house was connected to the motel. We had no neighbors, only transient guests. I was very lonely. We went to a cafeteria about once a week for dinner. When I was finished eating, I walked around the cafeteria and said, "Hi" to all the people there.

One time I met an old man who asked me to sit by him in his booth. He was very tall and slim, had a greyish-white, straggly beard, extraordinarily long fingernails, and wore a tattered, black suit that hung long on his elderly body. He had a leather coin purse and when he took money out of it, his hands shook. He had a distinctive

The Effects

From the earliest grades, I had trouble sleeping. I was exhausted most of the time. Sometimes it was because I had been left alone in the house and I was afraid that I would be attacked by someone. I slept with a hair brush for protection. I didn't choose anything more lethal because I figured the intruder would take a knife, or other weapon I chose, and use it on me. Nights that I wasn't left alone, my mind was filled with distressing thoughts, making sleep nearly impossible.

There was absolutely no similarity between my world and that of the children with whom I went to the private school. I was sure that everyone knew that I was an outcast—a product of a chaotic, drug infested, violent environment. My emotional development was uneven, my social development warped. Paradoxically, I was both a very young, emotionally insecure, frightened child, and a street-wise individual who had had adult sexual experiences.

I felt dirty, unlikable, and different from everyone else. I had no friends. I believed that my "badness" was transparent and I think I gave off vibes to keep other kids away from me. I had too many secrets to maintain. I also isolated myself on one of the green school benches because of pain in my genital area. This experience was too distressing and consumed all my attention. That was grammar school. I don't remember learning. I don't remember playing. I don't remember being happy.

Puberty brought the issues surrounding my abuse to full force. I didn't want to grow up and be a sexual human being. There was too much terror associated with that idea. A developing body, sexuality, guilt, shame, powerlessness, and being out of control were all one and the same thing...and I wanted none of it.

Once I started to develop physically, though, I seemed to attract boys and adult men who would fondle me, have me touch them, or want sex from me. My self-esteem was so low that I didn't know how to say "No," didn't think I had the right, thought that *that* was what my body was for, and felt that somehow I must have asked for it. My insecurities made it obvious that I was too afraid to tell. Someone was bound to be mad at me, and I couldn't bear the rejection—it would have been all my fault. I might hurt somebody's feelings if I didn't allow them to do what they wanted with me.

Puberty was just too painful an experience to allow to proceed. (In retrospect, I am amazed at how powerful the psyche is. I stopped menstruating even before any weight loss!) I was emotionally still eight years old. There was no hope of integrating the sexual aspects of my maturing body into me as a whole person, because I wasn't one.

Repeatedly, over the years, I had lost control of my body and my will—vital connections to my emerging sense of self. Nor was I immune to the social emphasis placed on a woman's body. Thinness was equated with self-worth, success, and social acceptance. At the time, the pre-pubescent, boyish look was in, i.e. straight hips, no fat—a total disregard for the normal female shape. In search of an identity, I was extremely vulnerable to this value system. So, when puberty and adolescence struck, (the critical developmental period of identity formation) I went looking for a sense of myself through my body and through control over it. After all, my body was the earliest identity I had. I went back to find it. The alternative, I believe, was to go crazy.

The Perfect Solution

One day I was walking home from school experimenting with a more deliberate walking style, and I felt a calmness inside. I had figured out a way to regain my innocence. It involved being deliberate in *everything* I did and thought. In a way, it was a great solution for where I was emotionally at the time—in search of an identity. This new plan necessitated that I stop and examine what I wanted in every situation in which I found myself.

It became a problem when I needed extreme control in all situations. No, I wasn't going to allow anyone to "feel me up" anymore. I didn't want that. But I was also going to dress very carefully, fold my collar just so, and walk with my heal touching first, my knees very rigid, and my posture erect. I was going to run between the two piers on the beach every day and do my series of floor exercises. I could only eat once a day and only after postponing it (mainly with exercise) as long as I could. In fact, eating was not allowed unless I had completed my exercise rituals and organized certain of my belongings in special ways. I carefully selected and measured portions of the same ("healthy") food day after day, chewing each bite a certain number of times and putting my fork and knife down between bites.

I changed my writing style by printing very neatly and extremely small. I also changed my tempo of speech and I chose when and to whom I spoke. I started withdrawing from people and feelings because I felt that I could maintain my path better without these interferences. I became extremely controlled in all areas of my life, especially those areas related to eating and exercising. With this new lifestyle, I started losing weight and defying puberty.

As the pounds came off, I began to feel cleaner inside. I still didn't have any friends, but my obsession with my body shape, weight loss, and exercise camouflaged my need for companionship. Instead of feeling like an outcast and undeserving of friends, my obsession allowed me to feel like I was rejecting them, instead. I didn't need them and, in fact, I was better than they because I was becoming pure inside from not eating.

I can see clearly today the choice I made back then. My body, my femininity, and my sexuality became the enemy because, if it hadn't been for these, those vile sexual acts wouldn't have occurred. I wouldn't have been prey to others who used my body—used me—to gratify their own selfish needs. The experience of guilt because my body had become sexually aroused by such "unacceptable" acts was tremendous. I truly believed that I was "making up for my sins," and becoming pure, by feeling the gnawing tightness in my stomach from not eating or from making special additions to my exercise routine.

I never learned to trust. I had shameful secrets inside of me that I would never dare tell anyone. So, no one could ever know the "real me." Relationships remained shallow and unfulfilling. I never felt connected to anyone. I didn't love or care for myself. I didn't even know of the "after glow" when I succeeded and the pain and sadness when I didn't.

When I moved to another state after five years of therapy, I was better, but not completely well. I had learned that it was possible for me to eat and keep the food inside, and I did feel better about myself. I was occasionally able to feel what came to be labeled as "connected" although it never seemed to last. Much of the time I experienced my body as being "shattered"—not completely lost, but the parts were disconnected from my heart and mind. I also remained ferociously angry with my mother but didn't understand why. I began putting it all together one night in a group I had joined in my new town.

The Understanding

It was the last five minutes. The topic must have been families or something. As I recalled mine, a feeling of intense hatred and disgust for Uncle Tony welled up inside of me. I said how much I hated him, unable to stop repeating it. I became wild and then suddenly sullen. Sinking from my seat onto the floor, I collapsed like a rag doll. I felt beaten, exhausted, with no will left. I was experiencing for the first time the emotions I had kept buried for twenty years.

I had been a member of this "personal growth" group for one and a half years, but I was too ashamed to tell these seemingly "normal" people that I was working on an eating disorder. Until that night, I had no feelings related to the sexual abuse that I had experienced as a child, and had convinced myself that this latter experience was irrelevant to my present state of unhappiness and not worth bringing up. Besides, I had plenty of issues to work on! I had low self-esteem, was uncomfortable around people, and couldn't break down and cry about anything. I was lonely, depressed, and came across as helpless. In fact, my appearance and demeanor were frequently described as "childlike."

But that night, I felt hatred as I had never felt it before. A woman in the group asked if Uncle Tony had sexually abused me. I nodded. Group ended. As I walked to my car, emotions flooded over me. I felt terrified, naked from exposure, and afraid of what was to come. Driving home I couldn't get the images and memories out of my mind.

Over the next several weeks, it became nearly impossible for me to sleep. Self-hatred and shame had been reawakened. Intrusive thoughts and memories of the past offered me no relief. I decided to try individual therapy again, this time with a male therapist, the group leader.

Sleep continued to be scant during those first few weeks of intensive therapy. I was afraid of something, afraid to let go, lose control, and dream. I was exhausted, running on empty anxiety, thinking about the past—things I had not thought about in a long time. Rather than anger at my abusers, though, I was feeling ashamed and embarrassed. What did those people in the group think of me? I felt so dirty. I wanted to hide and never show my face again.

The night before my third individual session, I did not sleep at all. I drove to my psychologist's office as though in a trance. His approach seemed different this time. There was more questioning, more prying. With a will

With this understanding came love and acceptance of myself, which enabled me to finally risk intimacy and thereby accomplish the final stage of my recovery.

Intimacy, Relating, and Recovery: The Final Stage

As an adolescent, I avoided relationships and intimacy because I didn't want anyone to get close enough to me to hate me as much as I did. As a young adult, I had sex because I thought it was expected. There was no relating, feeling close, or feeling love. I just felt used and trapped. I didn't know that I had the right to say "No," and feared I would lose whatever companionship I had if I did. Rejection, I believed, was worse than thirty minutes or so of feeling exploited.

As I came to find out later, I followed a pattern found in many other individuals with abuse histories who get involved with another abuser and repeat the past in hopes of making it go better this time, or who believe they are getting what they deserve. Thankfully, I got help and eventually became strong enough to sustain the uncertainty of being alone and starting anew.

As I came to like myself better, I was able to risk having others get to know me. I began to gain control of how much intimacy I got, and I stopped agreeing to sex when I didn't want it. This made me feel empowered. As I began to assert myself more, the intrusive memories of my abuse experiences were no longer being triggered, and they went away. This meant that I no longer needed the obsessions with food and weight to block out negative thoughts and emotions, and I stopped needing to starve to prove my worth and power, resulting in even greater gains in self-esteem and personal integrity. I began to feel free and strong enough to relate to others as *me*. Being able to "connect" to others was filling the void I had inside, and the empty craving for thinness became less and less intense. I felt more in charge of me, and therefore needed less and less to be in charge of food.

Inside, I began to feel and enjoy my femininity. My sexuality became fun, exciting, and something I got pleasure and satisfaction from sharing. Perhaps the most significant change in light of my abuse experiences is that I came to feel proud rather than exploited when my sexuality was appreciated and enjoyed. My partner was my lover and friend, not an extension or reminder of all my former abusers. I was finally feeling loveable inside and out.

A Retrospective Look and Today

Where did I begin? I got desperate—so miserable I wanted to die. Then I let someone earn my trust and I asked for help. I explored myself and how I got to be me. I wrote and read a lot. I learned to think for myself and challenged my beliefs. I tried new behaviors, and new ways of relating. And I kept on working.

I tried several therapists until I found one that felt right to me (this in itself was a sign of "wellness"). I worked through my experiences of sexual abuse—I remembered, I cried, I grieved. I understood my choices and I found no present relevancy for these. Towards the end, I concentrated on relationships, intimacy, and finally on learning to "parent" myself.

Recovery for me was like climbing a sand dune. The effort was continuous and tremendous, the progress

Years later I saw a photo of myself in my lovely, white Communion dress. The picture was chubby proof of how much I had indeed enjoyed that special breakfast, and many previous meals as well! But it would be years before I actually recognized that food and God were competing for first place in my life.

Lent

During my sophomore year at Catholic Central High School, God moved more obviously to the forefront of my life. It was Lent, forty days of prayer and fasting when the Church reminded all its faithful that Jesus had spent forty days of sacrifice and devotion in the desert preparing for His ministry and death. In remembrance of this, we too were called to make some sacrifice for the forty days preceding Holy Week.

More than once I tried to stop eating between meals and give up candy. I tried to stop bingeing on the hamburgers I snuck from the restaurant where I worked. I wanted to do it for God, and *secretly* I wanted to lose fifty pounds of fat. I knew that God loved me, even if the kids I went to school with laughed and teased. I was like Jesus, I reasoned. People spat on Him, called Him names, and made fun of Him as He carried His cross. My cross was to carry the burden of my fat and to accept people's making fun of me, while appearing outwardly to be okay—even happy. While I wanted to stop eating so much so I could lose weight, I thought that carrying my cross of fatness would be a good Lenten sacrifice.

My call to religious life came when I helped the Sisters decorate our church for Good Friday and the ensuing Easter services. While watching Sister Odarsa clean the

Sanctuary, I became transfixed by her hands as she scrubbed the altar steps. I was touched by her willingness to spend her life working for God and doing for *others*, instead of doing for *herself*. As I watched her, I decided that I, too, wanted to give my life and my work to God and others. I went home and directly to my room to meditate on the wonder I had just witnessed. A nun, in fact one of whom I was not particularly fond, had just presented me with a strong message—a calling from God!

I was so moved that I wrote a poem about the "Hands of a Nun." God seemed to speak to me urgently in that moment, "Come, spend your life with Me." I didn't hesitate. That night I made a firm decision to enter the convent and give my life to Him. With my secret vow made, I hurried from my room to the kitchen where I promptly prepared and ate two stacked cold meat sandwiches, washing them down with a tall glass of milk.

I felt excited, scared, and committed to move into the holy lifestyle. Feeling full and satisfied with my decision (and my sandwiches), I believed that from that day forward it would be God and me. I didn't realize it was really God, me, and food—*always food*!

Convent Life

After high school, I spent my eighteenth and last summer "in the world" preparing for life as a nun. I busied myself with the purchase of sturdy, black oxfords and floor-length, black skirts for my Postulancy (the one year probationary period of convent life). I ordered nightgowns (one size fits all) from Jameison's, the New York hot spot for religious garb. In a large, cumbersome, black trunk, given to me by my aunt and uncle as a high

During the long forty days of Lent we observed the ritual of eating two small meals, one big meal, and nothing in between. Naturally, I made the big meal a dinner fit for a giant. One Lenten Season, I decided to give up butter as my sacrifice to God. Daily, I put a small card at my place at the table. On one side the card had bright red letters spelling *yes*. That meant I had made it through another meal with no butter...yes for God! Side two said *no*, I hadn't sacrificed.

Finally Good Friday arrived. It was a solemn day. We wore our black cloaks in mourning to symbolize the death of Christ. That day there would be just two meals, a small collation mid-morning followed later in the afternoon with a Lenten supper. My Lenten sacrifice was almost over, and I had not had to turn my card to the *no* side even once.

Supper time arrived. The white fish and lemon pies were a community tradition. What symbolized Christ's death, however, were the generous servings of hot cross buns. As their aroma wafted into my nostrils, I grabbed two of the buns and slathered butter all over them. Without another thought, I crammed those buns into my mouth! Butter oozed from the corners of my lips as I swallowed the last morsel. Realizing what I had done, I slowly turned my card to the *no* side, dejected and full of self-loathing. I told myself that my cross—food and always wanting *more* food—was too much. I couldn't even sacrifice food for Jesus's death. I prayed to God, "Why did You give me this cross of fat to bear? It is getting harder and harder to carry. I can't even think of You anymore, God. The only thing on my mind is when and what to eat."

As I tried to bear my cross—wishing it away and at the same time believing I should accept it as God's will—God seemed to move further and further from me. When I was praying, I thought of food. While performing my Convent duties of teaching, or cleaning, or visiting the Parish, I was always waiting for the next meal.

Maybe God would come to me more clearly, I reasoned, if I tried some "spirits" of alcohol. In the secrecy of my early convent years I had pledged not to drink, but now I decided to throw caution to the wind. Besides the times they were a'changing. It was the late sixties, and my Sisters and my religious community were attempting to move more into the world of social action. In our efforts to be close to the people, we removed our religious habits and began to spend more time in the world preaching the "Good News" of the Gospel, offering comfort and support to the poor and downtrodden. However, as I moved into the world, I found partying—having fun singing and dancing! I also found the drinking man's (in this case, "the drinking woman's") diet—i.e., no food, just alcohol.

I did *not* find God, though, and after ten years of Convent life, feeling confused, lonely, unhappy, and fat, I slipped away from my religious community, seemingly without God, and certainly without the slim body for which I longed. Food and God remained my number one preoccupations.

The Dark Night of the Soul

At age twenty-eight I spent the first of many nights alone and scared in a small, one bedroom apartment. The job I found was a transitional one from the convent back to the world. In a small parish office attached to a suburban Catholic grade school, I coordinated the school's religious education program. I lived alone, worked alone, ate alone, and began to drink alone.

The days dragged by. God must be dead—at least for *me*—I reasoned. I cried and cried and cried. Drinking covered the pain of my out-of-control eating. Eating covered the pain of not finding God. Sleep became another drug, followed by my waking up to eat and drink again. I grew more and more despondent.

In desperation I finally reached out—not to a God I could not see—but to a human being, a Religious, a Sister with whom I had lived in the convent. Her life journey had not been one of perfection. She had not found God early in life. She told me that she was a recovering alcoholic who, as part of her recovery, let go of her childhood concept of God to embrace a Spirit and a spiritual life that used her own illness and imperfection to finally teach her about a loving, compassionate God. Her God cared for and could be there for all sick and weak children—including me. With her very *human* help, I gradually began to open the door of my spirit and allow bits of light to enter my soul.

With the help of Sister Florence's caring, I came to realize that neither God nor a spiritual life could be found in the "spirits" of alcohol. I stopped drinking and entered a period of long expectancy—of advent—of waiting for God to return to my life. I could sense Him at my door knocking, but I still couldn't find the key.

In these last efforts to control my own destiny, my dieting and eating patterns shifted into full throttle. I packed on the pounds until I wheezed to a crossroads in my life. I had to make a choice. I could ask for help with the problem that prohibited me from knowing myself, others, and God—or I could sink into the oblivion of the eating that drugged me as surely as if it were morphine.

Resurrection

Just as I had turned to a human friend in the pain of my drinking, I now reached out with the pain of my eating. Kathy, who was and continues to be my faithful friend, made a suggestion that profoundly changed my life—perhaps I could not find peace or the God who would participate fully in my life until I received help for my eating disorder. She explained that my eating had become an addiction and that until I stopped the cycle, I would never find God or peace.

When Kathy told me about a treatment program that would treat my eating problem as an addictive illness, the first glimmer of the resurrection of God dawned in my soul. My spirit, which had been lonely and empty for so long, began to rouse and bud with promise of new life. I now knew that I would seek and receive treatment, and hopefully, a different life!

In the structured protection of the treatment center, it took ten days to quiet the wild, obsessive voices within my body which demanded food. In this withdrawal from unhealthy quality and quantities of food, I felt shaky, hungry, and sick to my stomach. My tears were copious and my head throbbed. Emotions flooded over me and I was subjected, in the recesses of my mind, to full length movies of candy, chips, cookies, and sweet buns. I detoxed from food as if detoxing from alcohol.

As I completed my withdrawal from the toxicity of binge-eating, grazing, and sometimes vomiting from the sickness of a binge, my mind began to clear for the first time since childhood. I wrote a history of my eating behavior and stopped focusing on my weight. I began to understand that I had been unable to find God *or* myself because my life had been lived in a food-induced sedation that had prevented my being alert or aware of myself or others. Any connection with myself or my God had been obscured.

While in treatment, I tearfully read my history in a group therapy session. My hidden life of lying to myself about eating, sneaking and hiding food, and constantly bingeing and dieting was exposed. The courage and exhilaration of bringing my secrets into the open left me relieved and exhausted. I went to my room and fell into a sound and peaceful sleep.

Sometime later I was awakened by the tender, enveloping warmth of the sun on my body and feelings of safety and love. *God was there—outside me and within me!* As I lay there in that brilliant, all-encompassing shelter of light, I said aloud to myself, "Nothing has changed. Everything has changed."

I got up and stretched my arms and legs, appreciating my body and myself as never before. I rose from the bed and began to move about my room. Picking up the book, *Alcoholics Anonymous,* I turned to the story, "The Man Who Mastered Fear"*. As I made my way through his fearful life, I was astonished to read the following:

---

*"The Man Who Mastered Fear," *Alcoholics Anonymous,* New York City, World Services Inc., 1976, p.280.

'God, for eighteen years I have been unable to handle this problem. Please let me turn it over to you.' Immediately a great feeling of peace descended upon me, mingled with a feeling of being suffused with a quiet strength. I lay down on my bed and slept like a child. An hour later I awoke to a new world. Nothing had changed and, yet, everything had changed.

For a hair's breadth of a second, I entertained the notion that what I had read was a mere coincidence. That thought quickly passed, however, as I felt the chilling wonder of God coming to life in me and realized that this Holy and Loving Spirit had given me an extraordinary message through an ordinary event in my life.

From that moment, I was changed! I felt God's presence within. I began to pray and to meet God within myself and in the people, events, and activities of my daily life. I had searched for God in church, religion classes, the convent, and in alcohol and food, but in the gift of *freedom from compulsive eating* I had found a wonderful, spiritual Presence. I knew that if I continued to abstain from compulsive eating, I would keep on finding and knowing God in me, because I was finally clear-headed and alert—in both my body *and* my spirit.

Nothing has Changed - Everything has Changed

That special moment in the treatment center was a profoundly spiritual experience. Words cannot fully describe the shift that happened in the most still place in my soul. It was as if some secret door opened to allow a chunky child with a father who was a physician specializing in weight loss. Although paunchy himself, it was not *his* weight, but *mine* that signalled the need for immediate vigilance. The irony of my "problematic" weight and his profession was not wasted on me. I was not a good walking advertisement for him!

From a very early age, I was subjected to state-of-the-art diet methods—amphetamines at age six, a ten-day hospitalized water fast at fifteen, and a dizzying array of restrictive regimes in between. I grew up in the '40's and '50's, when dieting was not the household word it is today. I was the only person that I knew who was always either on a diet, failing at a diet, planning a diet, or rebounding from a diet. I opened my food deprivation "account" at age six, and continued making deposits into it for the next thirty-two years.

There is nothing like chronic deprivation and starvation to turn a perfectly healthy human being into a compulsive overeater. With each failed regime, my weight and setpoint inched ever upward and my metabolism became more deranged and less able to burn off fat. Of course, at the time, no one knew about setpoints and metabolic subtleties. Everyone, including me, thought I had no willpower, or some neurotic compulsion to be fat, or some gaping hole in my character. I, of course, believed it also. With each failure, my self-esteem plummeted, and my sense of deprivation and despair grew.

What I know today is that when we see disordered eating or people of size, we needn't go searching for deep neurotic wounds. We need only to look at the fat phobia that pervades our culture and affects all Americans. Our social values are especially merciless when it comes to women and our bodies. Cultural dictates drive us to feel disgust about our natural fleshiness; to devalue and estrange us from the wellsprings of our femaleness; and to pervert our relationship to food with prohibitions and fear. This is how I see it now: *It was dieting, and not some intrinsic neurosis, that made me into a compulsive overeater. Therefore it was dieting, not compulsive overeating, from which I really needed to recover.*

After thirty-two years of dieting failure, my resting weight was higher than ever. A lifetime of eating regimes had transformed me from a naturally chunky human being into a genuinely fat one. After one final fiasco, a 600 calorie/day "Quick Weight-Loss Clinic" diet that lasted for six weeks with a weight loss of only three pounds, I decided to give up dieting forever. I also gave up the ever-elusive goal of a slim body. I was delighted to find that once I gave up dieting, I also stopped eating compulsively.

The effect was not immediate. Recovering from thirty-two years of dieting required a process that would take several years to complete. It was a process of decriminalizing food, and of restoring my faith in the wisdom of my body. I needed to learn to trust in my own ability to self-regulate, and give myself permission to eat with pleasure. I don't mean the pleasure of stealing forbidden fruit that all dieters know, but the genuine pleasure that comes from listening to the body and giving it what it needs and wants when it needs and wants it, the pleasure that comes from self-nurturing and partaking of the bounty of the earth.

However, my legacy from a lifetime of dieting is that I live with what I call diet-induced obesity. Although I eat a moderate, healthy diet, and exercise fairly regularly, my

Had I grown up in the mainstream, I might never have been forced to develop my personhood. Perhaps it would have been easy to slide into the trap of relying on my beauty to get me through life. Who knows? I might have been a cheerleader or Miss Popularity. Maybe I would have married my high school sweetheart and cranked out a brood of children and would be home right now baking cookies and wondering how I was going to put the troops through college. Perhaps I would be stressed out as I watched my beauty—the very keystone of my identity—decomposing as I rapidly push age fifty. I jest and exaggerate of course, but the kernel of truth is that I would have more easily fit in with the stereotypical female role. I might not be actively questioning the value system that holds women imprisoned.

Conforming, however, was not an option for me, so instead, as I made my way through life, I highlighted my selfhood, my intelligence, my creativity and resourcefulness, my sense of humor, and my gifts of compassion and sensitivity. The most significant consequence of my own body struggles, the recovery it required, and the discoveries I have made in the course of that recovery is the work that I do. *The impact that has made on the lives of the many women it has touched feeds me in many ways that food never can.*

As I have gotten on with my life, my attention has been drawn to two issues: the fight for size acceptance, and the fight to save our planetary home. My sensitivity to both issues is a direct outgrowth of my own body history. The connection is obvious in the case of the former. Living in this society as a fat person—and a fat woman—has brought into clear focus the amount of prejudice with which people of weight are assaulted. This weightism or fatism—is a human rights violation that is societally rampant and yet nearly invisible because it is acceptable and pervasive. It hurts nearly all women—whether they are actually fat, or *perceive* themselves to be fat. I am certain that eating disorders will persist unless our society can learn to accept that human beings come in all sizes—by nature's plan.

My drive to do something about our planetary environment is also an outgrowth of my body issues, but is more subtle. It has become clear to me that our cultural abuse and devaluation of the natural world and of everything female are parallel abuses. The state of our relationship to nature and to our planetary home mirrors the relationship we have to our bodily home—something to be controlled, mastered, exploited. I think it is important for women—and men—to reconnect with values that are typically called feminine—nurturance, compassion, and a sense of relationship and context. We must realize the impact of present behaviors on future generations so that we can achieve balance at this very fragile time in our history and let go of whatever it is that holds women back from taking their role in this very important challenge. For many of us it is our troubled relationship to our bodies.

I once saw a bumper sticker that said, "A good life is the best revenge." Well, in spite of a highly "imperfect" body, I have made a good and full life for myself. I have a great deal of freedom to pursue what is important to me. I have a beloved family that consists of a husband whom I love and respect, and who loves and respects me, two absolutely wonderful dogs whom I feel very privileged to

Leap of Faith

Susan Kano

Over a dozen years ago I fought with myself, many times a day, over what and how much to eat—and in the end I never ate enough. Virtually every day I ran eight miles, or swam for an hour, or felt terribly anxious and guilty. And every morning I got my greatest pleasure, usually my *only* real pleasure, by getting on the scale to confirm that my weight was well under 100 pounds.

Today, I never worry about what or how much I eat. I just eat naturally and, for the most part, healthfully. I usually exercise three times a week, but if for some reason I don't manage to exercise, I don't feel anxious or guilty. I rarely weigh myself, nor is weight a problem for me. In other words, I have not only recovered from my eating disorder, I have freed myself from the diet/weight conflict.

Many people have asked, "How did you *get free* from the struggle and how have you managed to *stay free* for so long?" These questions aren't easy to answer, because my recovery was a gradual process which lasted many years. However, I can identify a key element of my recovery, a key without which I would still be "controlling symptoms," at best.

That key was a leap of faith into trusting and drawing strength from an inner realm. I resolved to trust my body's innate wisdom, particularly its ability to regulate my appetite and weight; and in an effort to cope with the resulting anxiety and pain which threatened my resolve, I went back to meditating twice a day, a practice which I had abandoned a year before becoming anorexic. Both spontaneous eating and meditation were essential to my complete recovery, and these two things continue to support my health and well-being today.

The Leap of Faith into Spontaneous Eating

I call the decision to eat spontaneously a "leap of faith" because the body's wisdom is not something one can touch, see, or quantify. I had to have faith that my body would regulate my appetite and weight, but there were no guarantees it would work. The mass media certainly didn't encourage faith in my body. Instead, it promoted self-control and thinness at any cost. Hence, I embarked on spontaneous eating with intense doubt, anxiety, and fear, and it took a leap of faith to proceed despite those feelings.

Knowledge based on research, combined with a lot of pain, led me to take this leap. I had read everything I could find about weight control, nutrition, and eating disorders. I had conducted three studies of my own: one of female body image, one of college students' attitudes and feelings regarding their eating and weight, and one involving two small groups of chronic dieters and bulimics. All of this research was, of course, another expression of my eating disorder; however, it resulted in a firm conviction that the human body has innate weight-control mechanisms which defend a natural weight or setpoint. I realized that ever since my first diet, I had been

111

engaged in an escalating, destructive, and hopeless battle with my own body. The only way to win was to disengage from the battle completely.

My leap of faith involved doing many radical and seemingly risky things. I strove to eat whatever I wanted, whenever I felt hungry. I stopped counting calories and didn't try to counteract periods of heavy eating with starving. I stopped weighing myself and stopped trying to be a specific size or weight. In short, I completely refocused my struggle. One day I was struggling to control my hunger and the size of my body, the next day I was struggling to listen to my body and eat accordingly. I had made the leap of faith.

My body's loudest message was clear: *Eat and keep eating!* If I craved a specific food, I ate it. Most of the time, I didn't crave anything in particular, so I ate a wide variety of healthy food in whatever quantity my body dictated. At the same time, I found that I felt better both physically and mentally if I exercised regularly, so I continued to exercise. I even allowed myself to exercise a bit compulsively (an hour of swimming five times a week), because my body didn't seem to object and the exercise helped to decrease my anxiety.

Of course, I didn't achieve spontaneous eating in a day. I took the leap into the process of change, and over and over I had to leap over the feelings, thoughts, and cultural pressure which stood in my way. But the process itself was one of slow, gradual retraining. For instance, I had to retrain myself to hear and respond to my body's signals. I had to learn to pat myself on the back for eating despite the temptation to feel guilty or to count the calories or to plan a fast. I had to avoid proximity to any scale—or suffer from an overwhelming urge to climb aboard. I knew that the scale was an enemy to my health, just as it had been an ally to my eating disorder.

The toughest challenge was allowing my body to find its natural weight, knowing that I would probably look and feel fat compared to the way I was before. I wanted desperately to choose my weight—or at least put a cap on it. Fortunately, I knew that this was not an option if I really wanted to reclaim my *freedom*. I might have been able to set a maximum weight, reach that weight, and then maintain it through chronic dieting; but, then the core symptoms of my eating disorder—the ongoing struggle with food and weight—would have remained. I didn't want to control symptoms, I wanted to be free of symptoms. I wanted to be able to eat in a natural, spontaneous way and let my body's weight-control mechanisms do their job. Therefore, I had to let my body find its natural weight no matter what that weight turned out to be or how much it hurt to be fatter.

Allowing my weight to rise to an unknown height was the most terrifying experience of my life. Intellectually, I was sure that I was doing the right thing, but my emotions kept screaming, "Stop this crazy experiment before it's too late!" Previously, my self-esteem and happiness depended on being extremely thin and on maintaining control, so I felt as though I was throwing away what little self-esteem and happiness I had left. Thus, my intellect and my emotions were at constant odds while I struggled to relearn a natural way of eating.

I wish I could say that after a few short weeks or months, taking the leap of faith was as easy as falling off a log. Quite honestly, it felt more like jumping off a cliff.

113

live with this lack of control over my appetite and weight. How could I live with my own powerlessness?

It's true that in order to take the leap of faith, I had to accept the fact that I was not meant to control my appetite or my weight, except through a healthy lifestyle. I had to let go and allow my body to do both of those things. Yes, I am powerless over my appetite and weight in that both are self-regulating. Appetite comes and goes as the body's needs dictate, and weight is, for the most part, genetically determined. But am I really out of control or powerless? I don't feel out of control now that my eating is natural and anxiety-free and my weight stable. I certainly don't feel powerless—quite the opposite. Although my weight and appetite take care of themselves, it is *my* body performing the feats of self-regulation, and its powers are *my* powers. Hence, I feel powerful.

The fact that my body has the wisdom to make me feel hungry when I need to eat and satisfied when I've had enough is both convenient and self-affirming. This form of control is far superior to counting calories eaten and calories burned every day in order to maintain a balance. The latter method is not only less effective, it's a colossal waste of time!

Only when you see your conscious self, your decision-making self, in opposition to your own body do you feel powerless. When you see your mind and body as one, as integral parts of the *whole you,* then you can allow your body to work without interference from your conscious self and not feel out of control. After all, it's *your own body* that's in control, not some other person or outside entity.

Birthing is a dramatic example of this principle. Some women emerge from the birthing experience feeling more powerful than they have ever felt before, while others emerge feeling utterly powerless and out of control even following a normal, successful delivery. Why? Because if you try you will find that you cannot control the frequency or intensity of the contractions, you can't even control when the baby will emerge! It's easy to find yourself wishing that you could stop or control the process—but you can't. Your body will continue to work on giving birth regardless of what you want. Luckily, if you are well prepared for this reality and you have good labor support, you can surrender yourself to the process and emerge feeling utterly victorious.

The respect I had developed for my body's wisdom proved to be very helpful when I gave birth to my daughter in 1989. I reasoned that since birth was a natural process, my body would probably know what to do, just as it knew how to regulate weight and appetite. I further suspected that unnecessary medical interventions would be destructive, just as dieting had turned out to be. Many books about childbirth confirmed my suspicions. Therefore, I found an obstetrical practice with a philosophy of nonintervention and I had a wonderful birth experience by stepping aside and letting my body do its job.

This is what the leap of faith is all about: recognizing the difference between things you should control with your intellect versus things best left to your body's wisdom. You relinquish control of your appetite and weight to a different part of yourself and thereby draw strength and support from an inner realm.

How is it that at thirteen years of age I had not only a healthy attitude toward my body, but a precocious dose of courage and conviction as well? This would have been a classic time for me to begin struggling with eating and weight, but I didn't do so until almost four years later. Furthermore, I didn't become *really* obsessed until I stopped meditating.

In retrospect, I can see big differences in my emotional health and general well-being depending on whether or not I was meditating. In high school and, initially, in college, I actually *enjoyed* school most of the time. I had a healthy social life. I had a lot of self-confidence for my age. I didn't feel any need to be particularly popular, "cool," or physically attractive. I didn't even use makeup or shave my hairy legs! But after I stopped meditating I became reclusive. I saw few friends and my tendency to work hard became an extreme case of workaholism. I became obsessed with my appearance and weight and, worst of all, I stopped enjoying my life. Now I feel that the worst mistake I've ever made was to stop meditating.

Conclusion

Our society, as a whole, doesn't seem to believe in an inner realm of wisdom. Virtually everything which requires a belief in that which cannot be touched, seen or measured has been rejected, while anything which seems to increase our control of nature has been enthusiastically embraced—despite negative repercussions. But for me, a leap of faith into an inner realm of wisdom, both physical and metaphysical, has enabled me to heal and to live a much fuller, happier life.

I am confident that *anyone*, even chronic long-term eating disorder sufferers, can break *free* from their diet/weight conflicts and not just "learn to control symptoms." This is not to belittle the control of symptoms. Any progress toward recovery from an eating disorder is a fabulous victory for the sufferer and his/her therapist and loved ones. But I feel that it is sad and unnecessary for anyone to settle for the control of symptoms. We all deserve to go beyond that victory, to real freedom. And for *that* to happen, we need to listen to and rely on our inner wisdom—wisdom which even many years of neglect cannot destroy.

I wish you good luck, good health, and happiness. I wish you the self-acceptance and self-love which you certainly deserve. And I hope that you will soon be feeling at home in your body, living in harmony with your hungers.

Rebecca Ruggles Radcliffe

The first time I met Rebecca Ruggles Radcliffe in person was at an eating disorders symposium in Phoenix. As she reviewed the notes for a workshop that she was about to lead, her two-week-old daughter, Chloe, slept cradled in Mama's arms. Here was the picture of maternal warmth and professional commitment, which reminded me of myself! When my son Charlie was eight months old, I brought him on a three-week speaking tour of New England, trying to balance altruistic goals and love for my new baby. I thought back to the challenges of that trip and wondered how Becky was approaching the same conflicts.

As I got to know her better, I understood how she has been able to accomplish career goals without compromising personal needs. She is an exceedingly positive person, cheerful and bright, while being sensitive to serious, broad issues. Having gone through intense periods of self-examination and personal growth, she is articulate about women's concerns and lectures nationally on body image, eating disorders, and related women's issues. She is the founder and executive director of Eating Awareness Services and Education (EASE), which specializes in education about eating disorders, and the author and publisher of a book entitled **Enlightened Eating.** *In addition to her work, she insists upon time for regular exercise and daily meditation; and as a single mother, she is absolutely devoted to Chloe. From*

Hunger for More

Rebecca Ruggles Radcliffe

I was born into a fairly ordinary Midwestern world—four kids living in a small town with college-educated parents who dreamed of providing a better life for their children. My family believed in hard work and measured worth by achievements. As kids, grades were important, and so was getting along with our friends, teachers, and adults. We were expected to understand how much our parents cared for us by the effort they made to give us the best—music lessons, braces, carpools to after-school activities, etc.

There was no clue in this quiet beginning that I was going to question my upbringing, purpose in life, and relationship to food. As my life unfolded, however, it took the form of a journey to redefine my self and my world; and on this spiritual journey I discovered that food was one of my most important teachers—a signal that told me when something was out of balance in my life or when something deep inside needed to be healed.

Eating for Comfort

My discomfort with my body began early. I began putting on excess weight at age five. I remember the humiliation I felt when I outgrew my tap dancing costume.

My mother ordered my clothes in chubby sizes. At family picnics, I felt ashamed and isolated for being fatter than I was supposed to be. I didn't think that something was missing or wrong. I just ate—a lot.

My family knew how to eat, and most of us showed it. Saturday mornings were spent plopped in front of the television eating bowl after bowl of cereal with my little brothers. Later, we'd eat our "real" breakfast with my parents and have pancake contests to see who could eat the most. My mother often made cookies and cakes to celebrate special occasions and to comfort us when we were sick or upset.

Sometimes, we'd join relatives for Sunday dinner and be encouraged to eat second and third helpings to show my grandmother our appreciation and love. We were praised for being members of the "Clean Plate Club" to help the starving children in India, forced to stay at the table until we finished our food. Late dinners were followed by bowls of ice cream and slices of homemade bread in front of the television with other members of my family. Eating was our expression of intimacy.

I was so out of touch with my body's hunger that I ate however much my mouth wanted. At birthday parties, I devoured endless quantities of snacks. At school, I would take several peanut butter and honey sandwiches because I loved them so much. I ate bowls of fresh-cranked homemade ice cream, piles of shrimp, and handfuls of cookies. By third grade, the other students called me "Bubbles." When it was my turn to be weighed, the teacher thought the scale was broken as it hit "100." I felt horrible. To top it off, I developed early, with breasts that bounced uncomfortably in fifth grade gym class because I did not yet have a bra.

I finally got fed up and took charge. I went on a diet. I cut out desserts, ate smaller amounts of food, and stopped eating bread and potatoes. Slowly, over the next two years, I grew taller and my weight moved into a lower range. By seventh grade, I was 5'4" tall and 122 pounds, but still felt fat compared to most of my friends who weren't yet developed.

I now thought I was "wiser" about how my body worked, and I developed a system of balance. If I ate a lot at one time, I would eat less later to make up for it. This relatively vague approach was guided by the numbers on my bathroom scale.

I continued to eat, however. I rummaged around the kitchen after school for leftovers, crackers, cake, tuna salad, peanut butter, and more. No one else was around. It was a very private unwinding ritual for me. I balanced this late-day eating by barely touching breakfast and having only a small lunch. By the time I was sixteen, that meant eating a single grapefruit. My weight remained the same, but so did the self-conscious, fat feeling I had about my body.

A Search for Meaning

My struggle with my body mirrored my internal struggle during these years. I began questioning everything, from my religion, to my parents' values, to society's rules. I was miserable, and it didn't seem fair or right to me. I couldn't identify what was wrong. I just believed that humans were meant to be happy, and I was not—nor were the people around me. Most of the adults I knew seemed to simply be going through the motions of their lives.

I started reading everything I could get my hands on that might give me insight about the meaning of life: science fiction, paranormal phenomena, Holocaust stories, philosophy, ancient religions, and self-help books. I joined anti-Vietnam War demonstrations, briefly experimented with drugs, volunteered in a literacy program, studied pollution, and eventually learned Transcendental Meditation. There was indeed more to life than my parents and teachers were letting on and my search gave me hope. There *was* more than one way to interpret truth.

Seeking out my own beliefs and values instead of blindly accepting those of my family, teachers, and religious instructors wasn't easy. The adults around me were disturbed by my rebellious and outspoken attitude. I felt like an outcast, but I stubbornly refused to give up. Each time I discovered a new way of thinking about God, life, or love, my commitment to go on trying to figure things out became stronger. I was driven to feel whole, and my suburban lifestyle certainly wasn't giving me any answers.

I moved out of the house at age seventeen. On my own, I shopped at the health food co-op down the block. Although I had adopted a Macrobiotic diet of whole grains and vegetables, I also stopped at the Dairy Queen for hot fudge sundaes. I didn't feel particularly uncomfortable about my body, because the counterculture celebrated the naturalness of all female body shapes. But the images of my Barbie doll and Twiggy had sunk deep, and in the back of my mind, I still believed that thinner was better. Even after a three week fast, I was the thinnest

I had ever been—105 pounds—and still thought my thighs were too fat!

That fast and my Macrobiotic eating took its toll physically. One day I found myself violently pushing through a crowd of people to find food—I was so shaky! I began to pay more attention to what my body really needed, and I quit skipping meals. I ate a healthy whole-foods fare, but continued to indulge in hot fudge, brownies, cookies, and other sweets. As of yet, I had no inkling of my emotional relationship with food.

The Journey Inward

The window to my inner world opened during the years that I went to college, started working, got married, and began a therapeutic process. I found out I wasn't who I thought I was! I had always pictured myself as an intelligent, confident, successful, and sensitive individual, and I was—but I discovered that I was also hurt, angry, and bruised.

As I explored this new layer of myself, I had to face an inner emptiness that I had not known before. It was deep, dark, and enormous. I longed for arms to comfort me. I wanted to be hugged or held while I cried. This was not to be—nor had it ever been. My parents' Scandinavian and British heritage spoke loud and clear in my upbringing. We valued dignity and stayed in control by using our intellects. We discussed matters of the world around us but never feelings. If we did get upset, it was in private, away from the sight of others. Preferably, we did not get upset at all. I was told clearly that people liked little girls who were happy and pleasant, not pouty, angry, or sad.

As I worked with my inner world, childhood memories surfaced. I now had emerging pictures to go along with the feelings. My parents read to me, gave me lessons, and took me to the beach. My family went to church together, visited relatives, and took sightseeing trips. But I was not held, cuddled, or hugged. I wasn't told how wonderful I was. I never heard "I love you" except on birthday cards. I grew up hiding behind the chair in my parents' living room, buried in a book, because it was the coziest place I knew. I escaped into a story to feel love or hope through its heroines.

Twenty-five years later, I had to learn how to face the past. It was not easy. My parents had unintentionally left me feeling unloved, unlovable, and brokenhearted; and I had been looking for this missing affection in every other relationship. I spent the next few years grieving each new realization of my childhood loss. I consoled the little girl in me who had been alone so long. She needed me to listen, acknowledge, and accept her feelings. This process of healing my inner self, although difficult, laid a sure foundation for the insight to come.

Connecting Food and Feelings

With my interest in human development, I became an educator. Over the years, I moved into health care where I helped begin and market new health care services. Because of this professional background, I was hired to help open The Renfrew Center, a treatment facility for eating disorders. As I met and worked with women seeking help for anorexia nervosa and bulimia, I was struck again and again by the similarity between the issues that I had been working on and those that these women faced.

make. Now as I turned inward to listen, I fed myself with attention. Listening to my deep inner feelings made me feel worthy, nurtured, and loved. I began to trust that I would always be there for myself.

The Courage to Question

This revelation radically shifted how I thought about the role of food and hunger in my life. Until now, I thought I had a healthy relationship with both, because I managed to keep my weight stable and within a socially "acceptable" range. Even though every Monday morning I vowed to eat less, I assumed that this was normal. Women simply had to do this!

I didn't realize that I had been shamed into trying to conform to the norm and was relying on willpower to keep me in control. Accepting this way of thinking made me hate my body and quietly eroded my self-esteem. The self-conscious feeling I had—and still sometimes feel— whenever I put on my jeans and go out in public, reflected the cruelty to women that is inherent in the obsession with thinness. Yet giving up dieting and accepting my natural body potentially meant profound isolation and loneliness. How could anyone love my round belly, big bottom, and thick thighs?

To get beyond this culture-wide system of thinking, I began to question again. Is thinner really better? Is there really only one body size or shape that is beautiful? Am I morally weak or ugly because I don't look like a model? Does this make me unworthy of friendship, attention, or love? Does it make sense that my self-worth should be measured by my ability to fit into a size four skirt? Questioning these assumptions was a constant reminder that growth as a person was more important than spending energy creating a "perfect" image.

Forming a new relationship with my body and with food were important steps in personal growth for me. I had achieved success in my career, traveled widely, lived in comfortable surroundings, and developed wonderful friendships, yet I still felt crummy about my body. My hunger and my body's remarkable ability to gain weight were my enemies. This left me divided within myself and rarely at peace regardless of any outward success.

Today, my choice to eat, both for fuel and for comfort, is conscious. This doesn't mean I don't eat when I am stressed. I do. When I am rattled about something, I talk to myself about it, figure out how to handle it, and identify ways to nurture myself. Even so, I may still want a brownie. This makes sense to me. Food still gives me a comforting, full feeling, so sometimes I choose to comfort myself with food, and I go get a brownie. But food is never the only remedy I use; and, if I don't take the time to listen, then I find myself eating more brownies more often. It can take me a while to "get it," but I finally hear my inner cry for attention.

The Ongoing Search for Wholeness

After several years of listening to my hunger and what it can teach me, I am even more convinced that my responsibility is to learn as much as I can about myself and gain truth from each situation. I move through my days with one goal—to seek more wholeness. I want to clean out every old belief that limits me. I want to get clear enough for my inner creativity to come forth. I listen closely to my emotional hunger to keep me tuned into

Caroline Adams Miller

I got to know Caroline Miller when my company published her book, **My Name is Caroline**, in softcover after Doubleday had great success with the hardcover. We have talked on the phone many times, and her ambition, dedication, and charisma never cease to amaze me. She has an uncanny ability to attract the media and has appeared on dozens of radio and television shows, been profiled in magazines and newspapers, and even had a letter and address printed in Dear Abby!

Since her book thrust her into the national spotlight in 1988, Caroline has worked with unceasing resourcefulness to help people learn about recovery from eating disorders. She has established the Foundation for Education on Eating Disorders (F.E.E.D.), served as a consultant for treatment facilities, and written a book of daily meditations titled **Feeding the Soul**. She has also taken her message to conferences and schools and personally answered almost 20,000 letters from bulimics who were inspired by her autobiography.

In her chapter, Caroline addresses how important it is to understand that food and weight-related behaviors are just the tip of the iceberg when it comes to healing. Fueling those behaviors are a myriad of personal and cultural factors, all of which need to be examined carefully. Here she discusses what she has learned in the areas of responsibility, spirituality, honesty, and motherhood. As always, she is frank and my life. Wrong. I was discomfited to find tidal waves of emotion crashing around me that left me alternately giddy and deeply depressed. No one had warned me that the hours I had once spent planning binges and eating would be replaced with raw, unprocessed feelings. After all, wasn't everything supposed to fall into place, bringing perfect peace, once I decided to stop bingeing and purging? Why was I now so angry and scared? I briefly entertained the notion that perhaps going back to the food—even with the side-effects of heart arrhythmia, swollen face, crumbling teeth and poor self-esteem—was preferable.

When I think about the odyssey of recovery, I am often reminded of the first line of M. Scott Peck's best-seller, *The Road Less Traveled.* He states quite simply, "Life is difficult." For me, and many with eating disorders, this is a revolutionary concept. I believe that we live in a fantasy world where we think we shouldn't have setbacks, sadness and discomfort—the stuff of life—and that one of the reasons we descend into food addiction is to hide from these realities and avoid dealing with them. It wasn't until I fully accepted the idea that recovery wouldn't always be easy that the benefits of feeling the pain of life outweighed the transitory numbness bingeing had brought me.

But this was a slow process that was hampered by my lack of emotional maturity. I found that as a newly-recovering twenty-two-year-old, I had the attitudes and wisdom of a pre-teen—the approximate age when my food obsession had taken over. I can think of countless situations in recovery when this immaturity reared its ugly head and retarded my progress, making the task of getting well seem unreachable at times.

In hindsight, my naivete was especially apparent in my decision to get married nine short days after graduating from college. Although I love my husband deeply and we have a wonderful, strong marriage now, I think I married him for the wrong reasons. For one, I had had a paucity of dates in my life and I was afraid that no one else would ever find me attractive. But most of all, I nursed a fantasy that marriage would provide me with enough contentment and self-esteem that my eating disorder would simply vanish. (When I got married neither my husband nor anyone else knew about the bulimia.)

My thoughts about marriage being a cure-all were grossly unfair to both my husband and myself. Although I soon confided in him about my eating disorder and took the initiative to begin recovery several months later, I subconsciously still viewed him as my "rescuer"—the person I could run to for solutions whenever life got hard. Instead of accepting that my happiness and self-esteem were dependent on what *I* did and how *I* viewed myself, I continued for a long time to hold him responsible for my well-being and contentment.

My inability to face life's difficulties emerged in other large and small ways during the early years of our marriage as I pursued recovery. For instance, I refused to deal with bills or my checkbook because that was "a man's job." If I had a conflict with someone, I allowed my husband to step in and mediate the problem; otherwise, I simply cut the offending person out of my life. And when dark troughs of depression hit me, I wallowed for days or weeks. If my husband needed love and sympathy, I'd be baffled. "I'm the one who needs attention," I'd think. "How dare he demand that from me!"

When we joined forces in business together, I allowed him to do most of the thoughtful, time-consuming work because I was afraid I wasn't smart enough. When I was ultimately forced through circumstances to take over the whole enterprise, I was terrified and angry. However, to my great surprise, I discovered I was quite capable and had I challenged myself earlier to learn new skills, I would have been proud of myself. This episode is what finally drove home to me the importance of taking responsibility for myself in every area of my life.

I wish I could say that I figured this pattern out by myself, but I didn't. Although I religiously attended self-help groups and read whatever books I could find on addiction and eating disorders, I finally sought the services of a female therapist who helped me clarify these issues and untangle my confusion. Just taking this step was difficult because of my independent streak and obsession with "What will others think if they know I'm in therapy?" My positive experiences, however, and the experiences of many of my recovering friends, have convinced me that unless someone is an unusually introspective and honest person, he or she will need a skilled, confrontational therapist at some point during recovery to serve as a catalyst for making permanent and difficult changes.

As a result of identifying my pattern of being dependent on others to get my needs met, I have spent much of the last few years focusing less on food than on taking responsibility for my own challenges, feelings, and goals. Now when I pay mortgage bills, change the oil in the car, rock a sick baby to sleep, and confront personal disputes, I feel myself growing up a little at a time. Yes, I wish I had done this ten years ago instead of diving headlong into food, but better late than never!

Developing a Spiritual Bedrock

In addition to learning to shoulder responsibility, it is equally important to develop a strong spiritual belief system—a quest that has preoccupied me since I stepped into my first self-help meeting. Early on, I embraced the idea that people with addictions are hungering not for food, money, sex, cigarettes, drugs, or alcohol, etc; they are trying to fill a deeper, yawning hole within. Carl Jung once said that anyone who is in crisis over the age of thirty is having a spiritual crisis. That made sense to me.

The self-help group for compulsive eaters that was primarily responsible for my recovery endorsed the idea of a "Higher Power." That was acceptable and non-threatening to me, particularly because I had never attended church—or even been baptized—and didn't think God knew who I was. My biggest hesitation, whether it was a specific God or a nebulous Higher Power, was the idea that I could rely on something unseen for strength and comfort. I did believe that I had made food a god and lost touch with the divinity of life, however, so I was willing to try to get in touch with whatever universal force existed.

My spiritual growth coincided with the explosion of the New Age movement. For that reason I allowed myself to get involved in a number of unusual practices I previously would not have given credence, like trance channelers, faith healers, metaphysical prophets, and goddess religions. This was, in part, a reflection of my "magical" thinking and reluctance to accept the ordinariness of life.

interest, surprise, and acceptance. I also can't even begin to count the times people have used the occasion to ask me for advice about what they should do about their own food obsession.

I've often heard it said that if someone is willing to lie about small things, he or she will lie about the big things too. In my self-help group I learned that committing to a daily meal plan and then following it was an important first step in creating an honest lifestyle. This was true for me. I went from being honest about my eating, to being honest with others, to being honest with myself about my character. When I completed the process of making amends to people I had harmed I felt I had learned the ultimate lesson in humility and honesty.

Maturing Through Motherhood

I'd like to share one last important experience I've had during the last few years that countless bulimics and anorexics worry about, but that hasn't received as much attention as other aspects of the disease: trying to conceive and then actually going through pregnancy as a recovering bulimic. When I first started to purge my food at the suggestion of two of my high school friends, I had no idea how many physical and emotional side-effects there were. If I had known, I might have sought help sooner than I did. But at any rate, at the age of fifteen it didn't occur to me that throwing up my food could potentially affect my ability to have my own family, which it ultimately did.

By the age of twenty-two, I had never had a menstrual period. I had never dwelt on this because as a competitive swimmer it had been a blessing. I also knew that athletes often competed with very little body fat and a great deal of stress, which could cause amenorrhea. But when the swimming stopped and my body still didn't respond, I began to worry. Despite the return of some hormonal normalcy after my marriage and a few years of recovery, I never truly felt like my body worked right.

Thus, when my husband and I decided to try to conceive, I wasn't sure what would happen. Many of our friends who had had children gleefully told us that they had gotten pregnant "on the first try," so we did our best to be hopeful. But we couldn't ignore the months that passed with no luck. We started to discuss adoption and whether that was something we wanted to pursue. My feelings of inadequacy and guilt about what I had done to my body skyrocketed. I also couldn't forget the fact that many of the women in my self-help group meetings often discussed their own miscarriages, infertility tests, and ovulatory problems. I thought that maybe this was the steep price I had to pay for my bulimia.

Then, when I had all but given up hope, I got pregnant. As much as I had wanted a baby, however, I had no idea how difficult the intense body changes that came with it would be. Almost immediately I was hit with morning sickness that lasted all day and all night for more than four months. I found myself waking up in the middle of the night and rushing into the bathroom to vomit. As common as this can be during pregnancy, I feared the frequent nausea would ultimately lead me back to my disease. My doctor had no words of advice for me, and neither did most of my recovering friends because they were either trying to get pregnant, or the weight gain and cravings had thrown them into full-blown relapse.

As if that wasn't troublesome enough, the foods that had worked for me in my recovery weren't viable any longer because I couldn't stand to look at most of them. For example, although I had incorporated salads, lean meats, and fruits as a large part of my pre-pregnancy diet, I found that just walking into the produce section of the grocery store or looking at packages of chicken could cause me to flee, totally nauseated. Experimenting with smaller, more frequent, meals consisting of unfamiliar foods—or items I had once binged on—was very frightening. I didn't even have the luxury of phasing this new existence in gradually, either. It had to be done all at once or I was going to starve and harm my baby.

My exercise routine also had to change. Although I had switched from competitive swimming to long-distance running to stay in shape, I had recently cut back on my running in an effort to be more moderate. Now I found I couldn't even do that because of the nausea and joint looseness that pregnancy engendered. I decided to just walk a few miles each morning if I felt well enough, and hoped it would be sufficient to keep me toned and healthy. After a lifetime of daily vigorous exercise, this was a major shift that caused mild physical and psychological withdrawal, coupled with fears that my body would be soft and unrecognizable nine months later.

There was also, of course, the scale. I had thrown out my scale more than four years earlier as part of leaving my weight obsession behind, and I didn't have the slightest idea what I weighed. The doctor needed to know, though, so I had to face that mechanical monster every month, which was enough to make me want to cancel appointments. I dealt with this problem by explaining my bulimic history and asking the nurses not to tell me what my weight was each month—only if I had gained enough for a healthy baby.

I became a bit of a joke in the office each month when I'd come in, stand on the scale backwards, and plug my ears (if I hear the bars sliding, I know where they're going). Although I may have looked goofy, it really helped. I never knew what my starting or top weight was, but I was informed at my last appointment that I had gained twenty-two pounds in all. A few days later I gave birth to a gorgeous ten pound boy and by my six week check-up, with no real effort, was told I was back to my previous weight.

My second pregnancy was very similar, but different in one important respect—I gained the same amount and had the same size baby, but for more than six months I couldn't lose the additional fourteen pounds. This frustrating period forced me to look hard at why it was so important to me to get back into my old clothes again and why size was still an issue. The most positive outcome of this time, however, was that I was gentle with myself about weight loss, I never starved or skipped a meal, and within a year I had a figure that felt comfortable on me and that I could accept. It's not the same body I had before having children, but I've learned to love the softness that comes with being a woman, and I don't have the desire to look like an adolescent boy any longer.

Motherhood isn't just a time of coping with body changes, though. It's a time of learning that infants and small children have needs that often come ahead of our recovery schedules. So my controlling personality had to loosen up and adjust to not eating my meals at planned times, not getting to my self-help meetings very often, and not always being able to exercise or relax when I wanted. This was disorienting at first, but the children have given me an entirely new focus that has been a positive replacement for my hours of working on myself. I'm glad I had the opportunity to begin and solidify my recovery before I started my family, though, because I can't imagine how I would juggle motherhood responsibilities with the all-encompassing energy that recovery initially demands.

Parting Words

I am convinced that bulimia is the most wonderful thing that has ever happened to me. Although I spent many years trying to ignore it, hating it, then wishing it had never happened, I see today that my eating disorder is what was needed to change my life for the better.

Whenever I speak at a college, high school, or professional gathering about what I've learned in recovering from bulimia, I stress that it has been the most difficult thing I've ever done in my life. While I'm grateful that there were many helpful people when I most needed them, I'm also aware that I'm the one who did the work and who pulled all the threads together that wove my tapestry of recovery.

Doreen L. Virtue

Like Caroline Miller, Doreen Virtue found support for her recovery at 12-step meetings, and is articulate and comfortable discussing her story. She has appeared on numerous television shows in order to bring attention to the seriousness of eating disorders, and has written two books, **The Yo-Yo Diet Syndrome** and **The Chocoholic's Dream Diet**. Today, in addition to her writing and speaking, Doreen is a psychotherapist in private practice in Newport Beach, CA, specializing in treating sexual abuse survivors who compulsively overeat.

Doreen herself struggled with bulimia, anorexia nervosa, and yo-yo dieting. From fourth grade until she was the mother of two children, she repeatedly lost and gained hundreds of pounds. She read countless diet books, tried each fad diet that came along, and had a closetful of clothes from sizes 5 to 15. Grade school classmates teased her with nicknames like "Skinny" one year and "Fatso" the next, fueling her feast or famine.

A self-described "major people-pleaser", Doreen did everything she could to meet the expectations of others, not realizing that it was at her own expense. This became particularly damaging when she moved into adolescence and the expectations she faced were sexual in nature. In the "exuberant thrill" of her budding femininity, she padded her bra and paraded herself, only to be grabbed and fondled by a stranger. She lied to her boyfriend to maneuver a date with a more "desirable" catch who turned out to be overly aggressive. Over and over again, Doreen tried to look and behave in ways she thought were expected, but which left her feeling embarrassed and rejected. The end result was often a retreat into bingeing and the safety of extra weight.

Her experiences illustrate how confusing relationships can be for young girls—and women—who are bombarded with messages about how to look and act in order to attract men. They learn that their appearance is often more valued than who they are inside and that expressing their own needs or feelings, especially anger or hurt, is considered pushy and unattractive. As a result, girls, who are more apt than boys to place a high value on being in relationships, become caught in a web of physical and emotional abuse, sometimes self-inflicted, in order to please and belong.

Doreen became a chameleon—changing herself to fit each situation—and in this loss of honest self-expression, she became a stranger to herself. In the course of recovery she discovered that she had to speak up not only for her ideas and feelings, but for the body she had tortured into conformity. She writes, "It had nothing to do with weight, I learned. It had to do with honesty."

As you will see in her chapter, Doreen is a great storyteller, with a light heart and a clear memory. She is positive and upbeat, and has been enthusiastic and supportive throughout this entire project. Although we have never met in person, I have thoroughly enjoyed getting to know her and think you will, too.

Whose Body Is It, Anyway?

Doreen L. Virtue

I began sprouting breasts when I turned thirteen. Like a car travelling from 0 to 60 in a matter of seconds, I went from flat to B-cupped overnight. And because my mind was focused on pre-teen girl activities like horseback riding and long telephone conversations, I didn't notice my new developments. That is, not until the new male attention forced me to notice.

I remember the first time a man whistled at me. I was riding my bicycle to the school playground, and a driver hung his wolfish tongue out of his mouth and swiveled his head lustfully in my direction. Frightened, a little embarrassed, and definitely confused (Could he be whistling at me? Is this a compliment?), I almost lost control of my sting-ray bike.

Heading home, my mind explored the notion of male attention. I had grown up in a traditional, middle-class, two-parent family. My parents kissed in front of my younger brother and me, but never showed anything resembling "lust" toward one another. My father, however, did have a huge stash of Playboy magazines in the garage. I had never seen him reading them, which must have led to my feeling naughty when, at age eight, I found and looked at those magazines. I remember seeing the models' bare breasts and wondering whether I'd look like that some day. I hoped I would, maybe because I knew it was valued by men like my father. What little girl doesn't want her father's approval?

The summer after I turned thirteen, my best friend's mother, who was a "Stretch and Sew" fanatic, made two-piece bathing suits for me and her daughter, Anita. These bright Hawaiian-print swimsuits had huge, hard, foam-rubber, built-in bras. When Anita and I tried on the C-cupped bikinis, we liked how they looked in the mirror, but the vacuous space between our nipples and the bra cup felt odd and uncomfortable. So, being industrious young ladies, we decided to solve the problem and fill the cups. But what to use? Socks? No, too heavy when wet. Paper towels or toilet paper? No, they would disintegrate in the pool. Clearly, we needed to stuff the bras with a waterproof substance.

Our final choice: plastic sandwich baggies. Five secretly bunched up inside each bra cup. Later, Anita's mother drove us to the big public pool at the neighborhood community college for an afternoon of swimming.

Anita and I self-consciously removed our swimsuit cover-ups and walked from our towels and sandals to the pool. We looked away from the staring eyes of boys, and even some girls our age who must have wondered how our breasts had gotten so big. Then Anita and I looked at one another and—splash!—dove in.

About two feet under the water's surface, our plastic baggies became little balloons, filled with enough air that they began floating out of our bikini bra cups. Anita and I tried desperately to push them back in place, but it was too late. By the time we came up for air, there were twenty baggies floating on the pool's surface.

The embarrassment of that moment, however, paled into a light-hearted memory compared to what happened next. After we scooped up and disposed of our bra stuffing, Anita decided to sunbathe while I stayed in the pool. Then, a boy about five years older than I, with nice blond hair and piercing blue eyes smiled at me. I smiled back shyly, wondering if he'd witnessed our plastic baggy fiasco.

He swam over to me and introduced himself as Rick, explaining that he was a regular at the pool, and asking how often I went swimming. When I answered that it was only my second time there, he asked me if I'd had a chance to check out the campus gardens. "Not yet," I replied.

"Would you like a tour now?" Rick asked with a big grin.

Flattered by the attention of such a cute boy, and genuinely interested in the gardens, I accepted his invitation. We walked there, in our wet swimsuits, about 300 feet from the pool. I was commenting on the fragrance of a camellia bush when Rick wheeled around, pressed his body against mine, and pinned me against the bush. He placed his large hand between my legs and squeezed my crotch—hard. Then he pressed his lips firmly against mine. I sputtered a cry of protest, which seemed to surprise him. In fact, as soon as I drew back, he dropped his grip on my crotch. His expression clearly conveyed a, "Well, what did you expect when you accepted my invitation?" attitude.

My freshman year of high school, I had plenty of male attention. I went on double dates with my friends and fell in love with Karl, a relationship which lasted for six months. Karl and I loved each other, and everyone at Orange Glen High School knew it. I was happy. Karl was a gentleman, and rarely strayed from trying anything more than a hand up my blouse. We might still be together if I hadn't succumbed to male attention once again.

John, the cutest and most popular boy at our school, sent word through Anita that he wanted to date me. Me?! John wanted to date me?! I could hardly believe it. But what about my steady true love, Karl? I couldn't betray him. I didn't know what to do.

John kept pressuring me to go out with him, and I was weakening. Actually, I would lose the ability to speak sensibly whenever this tanned, blond, football captain smiled at me, but the fact that he wanted me did something indescribable to my awkward and still-wounded teenage self-esteem.

Finally, I decided to go out with him and devised a scheme to trick Karl, which I regret to this day—but it happened, and it's an important part of my story. I asked Karl to come over to my house on the appointed night. We were in the living room talking when the telephone rang. It was Anita, and I pretended to sound flustered when I answered.

"Who was that?" he asked.

"Oh . . .," I purposely drawled. "No one."

Fifteen minutes later, as planned, Anita called again. For the second time, I feigned a mysteriously hushed and hurried conversation. Again, Karl, the ever sweet, but jealous boyfriend, took the bait.

"Who was *that*?" was his impatient question.

"Uh, no one!" I answered, equally impatiently.

When the telephone rang for the third time, Karl's eyes bulged just a little as I got up to to take the call. I continued my Academy Award-winning performance and it had the desired effect. Karl and I had a huge fight, because he assumed my evasive answers to his questions about the telephone calls meant I was talking to another boy. He left my house. Forever.

I tried to ignore my feelings at that moment, and concentrated on the prize I had just won for myself. I was now free to date John! I opened the refrigerator, ate half the chocolate chip cookie dough my mother had prepared, and went to bed early.

People looked shocked the next day at school, when Karl and I passed each other in the hallways. We had been known as inseparable sweethearts. Now, we didn't even acknowledge one another. My larger-than-normal school lunch helped soothe the regret and loneliness I was beginning to feel.

My date with John was set for the following Friday night, courtesy of Anita and her planning talents. I was to meet him and several of our mutual friends at his house, and we'd all go out together. I got there around seven, and five or six kids from school had already arrived. Some were drinking beer, one was smoking a cigarette. John's parents, very wealthy and successful, were away on vacation and had left him alone in their hilltop estate home for the weekend. I sat next to John on the couch.

that I graduated to eating bags full of peanuts and raisins, and lots more p.j. sandwiches.

For the next few years, my weight vacillated by thirty pound swings. When I met my husband-to-be, I was in a heavy phase. Once, I mentioned to him how beautiful my body *really* was, that is, when it was slimmer. "Quit teasing me and do something about it," he remarked.

I became increasingly miserable, sneak-eating and purging. My husband, who was abusing alcohol and marijuana, would tell me how ugly and stupid I was, and became abusive—jealous and controlling. He convinced me that no other man would want me. During one period, he was so paranoid that when I would drive to a store, he would calculate the time it should have taken and would be on the store's telephone, waiting for me when I arrived, always with the same accusation: "What took you so long? You must have stopped somewhere. You must be having an affair."

At one point, so I could save us money at tax time, I took a college course on income tax preparation. I was shocked to find I received an "A" on my first test! So, I wasn't stupid and incompetent—as my husband had convinced me—after all! During our brief marriage, I had completely forgotten my childhood academic successes, and had allowed my husband to shape my self-image.

I then pursued college full-time, and after receiving my first degree in Psychology, I went to work as a counselor at a local psychiatric hospital. I counseled the hard-core addicts and criminals, and could empathize with their compulsions by thinking about my own behavior around food.

At some level, though, I judged these addicts and alcoholics to be less than me. My arrogance masked the fact that they were doing something about their addiction, while I would turn to compulsive overeating every evening. One day, while listening to a heroin addict discuss his struggle to become clean and sober, the truth of my own situation struck me. I realized I was as much an addict—a food addict—as the man I was listening to, and I knew I had to get help.

I had attended a few 12-step support groups as a student (purely out of educational interest, of course!) and as a counselor. I had even been to an Overeaters Anonymous group once, and had dismissed its members as kooks. Their similarities to my eating habits had somehow escaped my notice. The first time I attended O.A. for *me*, though, I knew I was in the right place.

I came home from my first meeting and told my husband about my compulsive overeating. His reaction was a mixture of shock, anger, and disappointment. Somehow, my recovery program was threatening to him. He tried bribing me to miss meetings, offering expensive shopping sprees or elaborate dinners if I'd *please* stay with him. Some of his bribes were tempting, so I'd talk about my struggle with my group and sponsor. And I stuck with my recovery program.

What I learned, through painful moments in this journey, was that I was terribly afraid of rejection. So afraid, in fact, that I had turned into a major people-pleaser. I would smile and agree with almost anything, and would hide—especially from myself—any negative emotions, particularly anger. I realized that I relied on others' opinions of me for my self-image and self-esteem.

If men smiled at me, I felt okay. If they ignored me, I felt less valuable. If someone made a comment about my weight, I took it as gospel. I was completely unaware of my own thoughts and feelings.

As I swept away the cobwebs clogging my emotional system, I learned, step by step, that I could be honest with others and they wouldn't leave me. I also learned that I had a voice of my own, and I began to use it.

I remember the time I first discovered that important tool, assertiveness. Looking back, it seems like a very mundane example, but this was a *significant* breakthrough in my learning to be honest with myself and others. I was at a small grocery store, standing at the meat counter and patiently waiting for my turn. I was to be the next customer served, when the butcher asked, "Who's next?"

"Me!" shouted a woman who'd been behind me for about a minute. My old self would have stood there silently fuming over the injustice, but I remembered my sponsor telling me, over and over, that my recovery, even my very life, depended upon being honest with myself and others. So I spoke up. "Excuse me, but I believe I was next," I heard myself say. The woman apologized and allowed me to be served ahead of her. I felt like Sylvester Stallone in Rocky I—a victor! I had been assertive and the sky hadn't fallen on my head. After that, I became more encouraged, more courageous, more empowered.

I was learning to reclaim myself and my body, and have some control over my life. It had nothing to do with weight, I learned. It had to do with honesty—self-honesty and the courage to be honest with others. The end result was that I lost the desire to binge-eat because I was taking care of my emotions and taking care of myself.

It took some time to feel comfortable expressing my opinions, voicing my desires and preferences, allowing others to know the true me. I began trusting my gut instincts though, allowing an inner voice to guide me when I felt unsure, confused, or insecure. Gradually, I lost my fears of abandonment and criticism, and stopped feeling responsible for other people's actions or emotions.

All my relationships have been impacted by these inner changes. I am able to enjoy the company of other women without feeling a competitive tension. In both business and personal relationships with men, I experience connections on intellectual and emotional levels, instead of just physical levels. I no longer feel ashamed or defensive about being respectfully appreciated for being attractive. This is because I now love and respect who I am.

My previous fears and self-mistrust had locked me—my very soul—in a deep, dark dungeon. Inside that cold, empty place, I turned to food. But as I allowed others to know the true me, intimacy and its rewards—trust, comfort, companionship, love, inner security, and so much more— fulfilled me. I then lost the need to use food as a substitute. These changes have softened and quieted me. As the inner turmoil exited, an inner peace remained. I am free. At last.

Judith Rabinor

I was still lining up chapter authors for **Full Lives** when Judith Rabinor approached my book table at the International Conference on Eating Disorders in New York. Although we had not met in person, our paths had crossed over the years, and I knew her reputation as an author of academic articles, presenter at major conferences, supervisor at the Center for the Study of Anorexia and Bulimia in New York, and clinician at Holliswood Hospital's esteemed eating disorders program. For several years, she had been the New York State coordinator for Eating Disorders Awareness Week, an organization I have also supported, and she has regularly ordered books from my company. We were both enthusiastic about finally meeting.

When I told her about **Full Lives**, we found ourselves wishing that she had gone through recovery from an eating disorder and would therefore fit my author profile. Then, in her thick, sweet, New York accent, she said, "Wait, let me tell you what happened to me this morning," and went on to describe a scene of personal bodyshame played out in front of the mirror in her hotel room. I immediately knew that I had to expand my vision for the book.

Her story reminded me that, at times, virtually all women feel uncomfortable with the way they look, not just those with clinically diagnosed eating disorders. What's more, although chats about the latest diet or complaints about chunky thighs are as common as discussions about the *and poof! You'll look like a new woman! Much thinner and much younger looking, too."*

I am astounded. Why should I get this procedure? It sounds serious! Like an operation, a serious operation!

Suddenly I am outside in bright sunshine in front of my college dorm, talking to my mother and my college roommate, Arlie. "Should I go through with it?" I ask. "The operation? Do I really need it?" In unison, both nod affirmatively.

"Go through with it," they say. "Nothing wrong with looking your best."

In the shower at 7:00 AM, wisps of my dream come back to me and I begin to question. In my work, I write about the difficulty women have feeling powerful and how societal values reinforce the notion that beauty is a woman's power. I argue that true power is achieved by forging a genuine self and identity, a process achieved through emotional and spiritual struggle and growth. In completing my article, I have accomplished a task which could—should—empower me. Yet in my dream, I squirm, and quiver, feel shriveled and powerless. I know only too well there is an intrinsic honesty in dream metaphors which I dare not ignore. What is the imagery of my dream telling me?

Details of the dream stayed with me all day. Images, thoughts and feelings surfaced and resurfaced in unexpected configurations. "Operation, operation, operation," hummed a little voice in my head, and as the voice got louder and clearer, I felt a sadness seep into me. The face and words of Ann, a thirty-nine-year-old client, emerged:

> *"The operation was more than I had antici-*
> *pated," she said, and began to cry softly. I*
> *wanted to weep. A long moment followed.*
>
> *Looking and sounding exhausted, she went*
> *on to describe the stomach suctioning in detail:*
> *incision, stitches, numbness, lingering paraly-*
> *sis, how they had removed layers of fat, ex-*
> *pelling fat cell after fat cell. There had been un-*
> *expected complications—inadequate oxygen*
> *caused breathing problems. I found myself re-*
> *pulsed by the hideous details of the invasive*
> *medical procedure and overwhelmed by the*
> *psychic pain she was recounting. My head and*
> *throat felt tight. As I held back tears, I won-*
> *dered how deadening myself might impact her.*
>
> *I remembered our conversation a week be-*
> *fore the operation. "What if I don't look bet-*
> *ter?" she had questioned.*
>
> *"What if you don't?" I had asked,*
> *somewhat frightened for her. How could she*
> *look much better? There was nothing that*
> *needed 'fixing' in the first place!*

Brilliant, witty, vice president of a nationwide chain of retail stores, she had started therapy hoping to save her faltering third marriage. But therapy moved too slowly. No quick fix. No magic cure. So she decided that what stood in the way of her having the right relationship were the legacies their own lives had taught them—that looking good is what really matters. Standing on the brink of achieving recognition and power, I had become scared, and from that scared place, the voice of my unconscious emerged, warning me of the danger of female power. Being powerful in this new way was too frightening to acknowledge, and so I resorted to what I had learned from my mother and grandmother: to do what was safe, acceptable, and traditional—focus on my body.

Woman Therapist as Bodyself

Recent theories of child development stress that it is through experiences and relationships with caretakers—mothers, fathers, and significant others—that a sense of identity develops. Familial and cultural traditions and values are passed, implicitly and explicitly, from parent to child, enhancing or impairing one's sense of self.

Formed in relationship, the self is also healed in relationship and for this reason—psychotherapy offers a client a second chance for growth. When the client peers into a new mirror, she will hopefully come to see, understand, and experience parts of herself previously unknown, hidden, unloved. The eyes and reactions of the therapist can provide such a mirror. So can the body, if the bodyself is present.

Early in my training, I learned that the most powerful tool of the therapist is the self. However, as I became more aware of my self as consisting of mind, body and soul, of which mind and soul were present in my office, I wondered, where was my body? Where was my bodyself? Why was I so silent about *my* body?

Why did I feel so uncomfortable letting clients know that I, too, had intense feelings about my weight, my fat, my thin, my thighs, my jiggly ass? Rarely, if ever, did I mention that I too, liked looking good, hated looking bad (which generally was translated into looking or feeling fat), and that my feelings about my body deeply impacted my self-esteem. On this topic I was practically mute. What compelled me to be so silent, or at best, assume a neutral posture when it came to even mentioning my dieting or feeling fat—subjects which obsessed and tormented my clients and stymied their growth? I began to think about my work. What would it mean for my bodyself to be more present? Could I dare share my feelings about my body with my clients? Which feelings? With which clients? Or should I remain silent?

I realized that although I believed that body dissatisfaction is normative and that female body image problems are ubiquitous, I was in hiding. While I, as a therapist, felt comfortable normalizing a wide variety of life experiences, such as the euphoria of falling in love and the pain associated with death, divorce, and loss, normalizing female body dissatisfaction was not part of my professional *modus operandi*. When a client spoke of body hatred, my job was to focus on her underlying problem, on her deeper issues which needed clarification. My role as psychotherapist both protected and sanctioned my hiding place.

Never mind that a negative body image was normative. Never mind that my own values dictated that being genuine and authentic with my clients seemed the hallmark of a good therapeutic connection. Never mind that acknowledgment of the universality of body shame might be healing. Never mind what *I* was learning about the connection between my bodyshame and my fear of personal power! When it came to the bodyself, a curtain of therapeutic anonymity automatically fell.

Self disclosure, I had been taught, was problematic. Therapists were advised to proceed cautiously. Only after much self-reflection and "working out" or "working through" their own issues could one effectively counsel clients. This puzzled me, for my impression of female colleagues' experiences in this area repeatedly revealed the universality of bodyshame. What's more, the professional literature generally indicated that therapists who had not worked out their own body image issues could not be effective healers. Burdened with the notion that their own bodyshame would impair their ability to be good therapists, shame about bodyshame was further silencing!

I began to ask myself new questions. Have therapists working with women with disordered eating "worked out" their own body image issues? Can healthy body image development be fostered in a culture in which body shame is normative? How can we, as therapists, foster body comfort in a culture which discourages body comfort, when our own bodies are a source of pain? I wondered how my colleagues felt about their bodies. Did they suffer with body shame? How did they deal with it clinically?

Increasingly, I came to believe that the silence of the therapist was at least confusing, possibly damaging.

Ending the Silence: Therapist in a Green Bikini

I began meeting with colleagues to explore how clients' body image issues impacted therapists, and also how therapists dealt with their own feelings of bodyshame. I developed a guided image exercise where the following situation was presented:

> *Imagine it is the first day after your summer vacation. Jane, bulimic for seven years, enters your office, sits down, and opens the session with, "Was that you I saw at Jones Beach this summer?" You wait. She persists. "July fourth weekend...was that you on the beach?" You pause, trying to remember exactly where you spent the first weekend in July. "Was that you wearing a green bikini?"*
> *How do you think you might respond?*

Responses from psychotherapists indicated deep feelings of anxiety, awkwardness, discomfort, and competition, and repeatedly revealed the ubiquitous nature of body image problems in female therapists. What's more, examining bodyshame in a group was healing. While self disclosure was at first anxiety provoking, over time, such revelations were comforting. Most therapists expressed relief to hear their colleagues also suffered from body image dissatisfaction.

I began wondering that if it helped my colleagues to know others shared their feelings, wouldn't it help my clients to have their feelings validated by my experience as well?

Nowhere is there a greater opportunity for a client to identify with me, her female therapist, than through our physical sameness, our bodyselves. Preoccupied with her fear of fat and her shame about her body, my client will at first relate to and evaluate me, her therapist, using the body as a yardstick. She will wonder about me, whether I diet, whether I am satisfied or dissatisfied with my body.

It is initially by addressing these body issues that obsess and preoccupy her—her thighs, her dieting—that I have a unique opportunity to develop, expand and deepen our relationship. By talking to her about *her* concerns, by listening carefully, by validating her fears (which at first are condensed and articulated only in her fear of being fat), I can begin to build a healing relationship. Eventually we will have the opportunity to examine how issues of weight, dieting, and appearance mask other, deeper issues.

In the beginning of our relationship, then, I must support her perceptions and validate her experiences. One way to do that is to share some of my own.

My approach to making initial contact with clients began to change. I became less interpretive, more symptom focused, and more centered on the body. "You're right," I found myself assuring Maria, an overweight client. "In general, being thinner makes life easier. I, too, hate feeling as though I am judged by my appearance or that I am not perfect enough."

I pointed out how easy it is for a body focus to develop and how even I am affected. Using myself as a role model, I taught clients to become aware of how this body focus is a distraction from other hungers. I tell them, "Sometimes I change my clothes ten times before I go out or eat when I'm not hungry. These are both *clues* that let me know that there's something else bothering me."

Most clients are relieved to hear that I understand and share their concerns. Likely to idealize me, many think I am immune from body issues, or that "normalcy" means total freedom from the pressure to be thin. But I explain that even though I am neither anorexic nor bulimic, I too watch the "I Feel Fat Show." By acknowledging and sharing this with my clients, I am opening the doors to mutual, honest, and genuine connections. For instance, by addressing how and what I have learned about my fear of my own personal power, I am exposing myself; but, I am also modeling courage, strength, perseverance, and compassion.

Over time, the scope of my therapeutic inquiry broadened and expanded. I found myself addressing the powerful social pressure to be thin and the political ramifications of that pressure. I talked about how society devalues women's achievements while glamorizing their bodies. I discussed the power of advertising and media messages which create a deafening inner voice that shouts of body and self hatred, and prevents us from listening to our inner needs, appetites, and desires. I talked about the process of recognizing how tunnel vision on one's body obscures the development of a genuine self.

Throughout this entire process, I acknowledged my own dilemmas struggling with powerful cultural factors, hoping to serve as a role model of a woman in touch with her needs, who is willing and able to feed herself, literally and metaphorically, and who struggles with cultural pressure which inhibits both.

A New Kinship

Repeatedly I am struck with the awareness that when it comes to bodyshame, we women—young and old, therapists and clients, mothers and daughters, fat and thin—are more alike than different. While perhaps less intense and less frequent, body hatred is familiar to me on a personal as well as a professional level, for the relentless pursuit of thinness dominates not only the minds and lives of clients with anorexia nervosa and bulimia, but insidiously infects the thoughts and feelings of almost all women in our culture.

As female therapists, we are not only guides and mentors, we are also companions and kindred souls, working with issues of powerlessness masked by disordered eating. Listening to our own "I Feel Fat Show" is one of our most useful tools, yet our bodyshame may impair our ability to listen, and hinder our capacity to use our bodyselves to reach out and connect.

If we are to model the reality of womanhood, which includes for most of us experiencing the struggle for identity in our bodies, and if we are to provide a vision for healing, we must be willing to reveal our wounds, our sorrow, to expose our bodyshame. We must be willing to challenge the traditional therapeutic model and give up the position of silent privilege. We must do what we demand of our clients: take risks, be authentic, be vulnerable, and speak up.

Kim Lampson Reiff 🌿

S*eated next to Judith is another dedicated psychothera-*
pist, Kim Lampson Reiff. Her book, **Eating Disorders:**
Nutrition Therapy in the Recovery Process, *which was co-*
authored with her husband, Dan Reiff, is a comprehensive
text and is widely-acclaimed by clinicians in the eating dis-
orders field. I became aware of Kim's work through "The
Hopeline", a newsletter based on her own experiences with
anorexia nervosa and bulimia, which she wrote and dis-
tributed in the early 1980's. We found out about each other
because her newsletter and my original booklets were often
featured in Jean Rubel's "ANRED Alert". We met several
years later when I joined the board of directors of Eating
Disorders Awareness and Prevention, of which Kim was
President.

Although the motto "Perseverance Overcomes" was one
that Kim applied to all aspects of her recovery, it was particu-
larly relevant to her learning about intimacy. Being close to
others can be extremely difficult for someone with eating or
weight issues because, as Kim writes, the "relationship with
food becomes a way to recreate a sense of closeness...or ex-
perience a sense of companionship and safety for the first
time." Giving that up in exchange for the vulnerability and
uncertainty that are inevitable in relationships with people
can be extremely scary.

An example of this recently came up in my own life
when a friend of mine who has suffered with anorexia for

twenty years asked me to trim her hair. As I lifted the rows between my fingers and gently snipped with the scissors, I knew I was the first person, besides a doctor, to have touched her thin body in years. Yet, with trembling legs she stood there, knowing that the safety of her obsession with food was just an illusion, and that her trust in me was secure. Never have I been more acutely aware that an eating problem is a form of protection from feelings of rejection and worthlessness, past as well as present, and that learning to love and be loved is a gradual—but powerfully healing—process.

Kim and I have collaborated on several projects over the years, and I have seen how committed she is to mutually fulfilling relationships—she gives the best of herself and sees the best in others. I have also had the pleasure of sharing her and Dan's family life at a breakfast in New York City during the International Conference on Eating Disorders. Their daughter, then two-year-old Krisanna, struck up a friendship with me that has lasted to this day—evidence of the love in her household. With appreciation for her perseverance and courage, I am pleased to introduce Kim's chapter.

Perseverance Overcomes

Kim Lampson Reiff

*If words could be unwritten and songs could be
unsung,*
*If rivers could run backwards and wrongs
could be undone,*
*If the wisdom that comes only with the experi-
ence of years*
*Could be learned in some way other than by
crying one's own tears,*
*Our stories would be different, the scars left
would be few,*
*If only we had known back then the things that
no one knew.*
*But on this note of sadness, the story does not
end,*
*For love and truth do triumph and the broken-
ness does mend.*

— *Kim Lampson Reiff*

My husband, Dan, once made the observation that
people who have eating disorders are actually recovering
from *two* sets of unhealthy behaviors: those that have to
do with food and weight and those that have to do with
intimate relationships. I think he is right. Somehow, in the

process of developing an eating disorder, they find that their relationship with food becomes a way to recreate a sense of closeness they once had or allows them to experience companionship and safety in a relationship for the first time. However, a relationship with an inanimate object, albeit non-threatening in many ways, does not satisfy the need for intimacy with people that we all have. Thus, I believe there are two significant challenges in the process of recovering from an eating disorder. These are: overcoming the emotional obstacles to intimacy, whether they be hurt, shame, anger, betrayal, lack of forgiveness, abuse, or ignorance, and then learning how to build healthy, intimate relationships with family and friends.

Intimacy and Food

I did not have a traumatic childhood. There were no major crises, no family members who were alcoholics, and no incidents of physical or sexual abuse. I believe I became vulnerable to developing an eating disorder when the cumulative effect of a number of factors resulted in my experiencing emotional pain and stress at a level of intensity greater than I knew how to manage in a healthy way. My limited ability to recognize and express feelings directly and my ignorance regarding how to develop healthy intimate relationships made it difficult for me to be truly close to people. Low self-esteem, stress (I was away from home for the first time and had to make major decisions on my own), and some difficulties my family had in communicating were other issues I was trying to resolve without much success. I remember focusing on my body much of the time, believing that if I could control how much I ate and become really skinny, everything would be okay.

It was while I was a sophomore in college that I developed anorexia nervosa and bulimia. For me, as is true for many others, the hurt I felt following rejection in a romantic relationship was too much for me to handle when added to all the other stress in my life. I remember feeling devastated, worthless, unlovable, and *too fat*. The way that relationship ended was so painful for me that I did not talk to anyone about it. I buried my feelings and had a "secret" for the first time in my life.

Having never heard of anorexia nervosa before, I found out much later that I was one of many who had unconsciously stumbled upon this ingenious, yet self-destructive, method of coping with painful emotions and hard times in life. I did not realize at the time that the obsession with food, the behaviors that went with it, and the extremely low body weight protected me from having to be vulnerable in relationships with people, especially men. My primary relationship became my relationship with food. If people hurt me, I did not allow it to bother me, finding consolation in the fact that I was thin— something no one could take away from me.

I spent the first two years of my eating disorder in denial. Public awareness about eating disorders was so minimal at that time that most people, myself included, were ignorant of their existence. However, when articles about anorexia nervosa started to appear in magazines and newspapers, friends suggested to me that perhaps I was anorexic—to which I responded vehemently that I was not. Without telling anyone, though, I read these articles too, experiencing an odd mixture of fascination and fear, as someone else's words described my behaviors with food and my feelings about my body and myself.

I do not remember how I first became aware of the book, *The Golden Cage,* by Hilde Bruch, but I do remember checking it out of the library and staying up all night reading it, transfixed by the words on the pages. One sentence had such an impact on me that I felt as though the words had burned themselves into my brain. That sentence was a turning point in my life and the start of my recovery process. What it said to me was that a person with anorexia nervosa spends all of her time, energy, and thought in the pursuit of something—namely being very thin—that accomplishes absolutely nothing of eternal value.

I knew in my heart that those words spoke the truth and this really bothered me. I could not reconcile my self-focused, narrow, eating disorder lifestyle with my faith and those things I believed to be important, such as being able to touch the lives of other people in a loving and meaningful way. That night, filled with an intense curiosity to find out why I had developed my eating disorder, I decided to recover no matter how long it took or how difficult the road would be.

Without conscious awareness, I was applying the motto which is written on a coat of arms which hangs at the foot of the stairs in my childhood home. It is a collage of hand-appliqued pictures, each of which symbolizes a significant period of my father's life as a single man. These pictures include: an anchor, which represents the time he served in the Navy; a clam, which reminds him of the years he spent as a professional clamdigger; an airplane, which signifies his experiences as a pilot; and the emblems of the universities from which he graduated. As a child, I loved looking at the pictures, but they were not what impacted my life—it was the inscription that was beautifully embroidered in black letters at the base of the coat of arms, "καρτερία ηίκα," which is Greek for "Perseverance Overcomes."

I cannot remember how old I was when I first understood the meaning of those words or when I embraced them as my motto, too, for it is as though they have been part of my thoughts for all of my life. From a very young age, my parents communicated by their words and actions that no problem or challenge would ever be too great for me to conquer if I worked hard and long enough. This philosophy has influenced me throughout my life. At the times of greatest despair while recovering from my eating disorder, I would remember the words, "Perseverance Overcomes," and find comfort, hope, and the courage to go on.

After nine years of hard work, I completed my recovery process. I found the changes in behavior to be more difficult than facing the underlying issues and emotional pain, but I chose to do both in order to be fully recovered. I find it remarkable that it took me ten months to lose forty pounds and nine years to gain thirty-five of them back.

Regaining that weight, which would appear to be so simple, was one of the most challenging accomplishments of my life. It took an incredible amount of perseverance, as did changing at least one hundred food or weight-related behaviors that I had developed over the years. With great difficulty, I slowly learned to eat normally again, without counting every calorie, measuring my food, eating only "safe" foods, panicking if I did not know the ingredients in a casserole or dessert, or dining only at restaurants with salad bars. I found it possible to stop drinking liquids all day to stave off hunger and to quit chewing gum compulsively. I no longer restricted calories as my weight climbed higher.

While severely anorexic and bulimic, I recall questioning whether anything good could come out of something so painful, frightening, and lonely. In my case, not one, but many good things came out of recovering from an eating disorder. I learned to value and appreciate my body and became strong enough to resist cultural pressures to look a certain way. While engaged in eating disorder behaviors, I felt as though I had lost control of my body (although in reality I had not). While recovering, I reclaimed that power and accepted responsibility for my body's care.

Two of the most exciting outcomes of my recovery were that I overcame my fear of being close to people and I acquired the skills needed to build healthy, intimate relationships. As part of that process, I learned to recognize and express my feelings with words rather than through actions or food behaviors. Becoming aware of new ways to face and resolve conflicts with others opened doors to closer relationships with friends and family, and intimacy became less of a mystery. My mother, father, and I grew closer in a healthy way after struggling with hard issues together. I also experienced the unconditional love of God which freed me to examine my weaknesses and imperfections without fear of rejection or judgement.

Although I consider myself to be a capable, reasonably intelligent person with a strong faith and a loving family, it still took me almost a decade to finish my work. In the process, I proved to myself that perseverance does indeed overcome adversity, and I knew if I could recover from an eating disorder, I could face just about anything.

Intimacy and Marriage

When I was in my late twenties, professionally accomplished, yet "still single," a significant phone conversation with my father took place. I can see so clearly where I sat that it could have happened yesterday—a small, second story room full of windows which I used as my study. I was sitting in a big, comfortable chair in the corner looking out at the tops of some beautiful trees. Tears were running down my face as I told my father that I was really lonely and thought I would never be married. Not the biggest crisis in the world, but a crisis to me, nonetheless.

Pursuing my career had been quite compatible with having an eating disorder, pursuing an intimate relationship was not. Although I longed for a relationship with a man, I was so blinded by my distorted body image that I was unable to see that my skinny body had for many years made me look more like a twelve-year-old girl than a woman whom a man would find attractive. At the time of this conversation however, I had gained a significant amount of weight, was no longer preoccupied with food, and felt more than ready to be involved with someone.

Expecting words of reassurance to the effect that my white knight was on his way, I was shocked to hear my father calmly say, "Little one, when you get married, you exchange one set of problems for another. Life is full of challenges. You need to learn to face them while appreciating the joyful times in between."

"But Papa!" I protested. I did not want to believe him. I did not want any more problems and challenges. I wanted a storybook romance. After I hung up the phone, I wanted to forget his words, but I knew I would remember them always. Now, I am grateful he spoke the truth because I have applied that truth to all of life, including recovering from my eating disorder and becoming a wife and mother. My father had gently confronted me with the reality that regardless of circumstances, there will always be a mixture of good times and hard times, and that it is *my response* to life's challenges and joys that determines if I will be successful and resilient in the face of inevitable periods of adversity.

It was shortly after this conversation that I met Dan Reiff. I had already worked on my recovery for eight years and felt quite proud of my progress. I was not only resistant to further altering food or weight behaviors when our relationship started, but I was tired of introspection and personal change. Much to my dismay, shortly after we met, Dan said I still "looked like" I had an eating disorder.

We were sitting across from each other in my office one day after work. He hesitated as he told me that he thought that my weight was still too low. Instantly defensive, I said, "It is not! No one else thinks that but you. I have gained twenty pounds and am not going to gain any more weight!"

The intensity of my reaction betrayed me. I knew he was right, but did not want to admit it either to him or to myself—although I did. It seemed so hard to have to face this issue again, but I was willing to persevere once more.

As I saw the few remaining ways I limited my food intake disappear, I felt in harmony with my body for the first time in many years. The freedom that came with being able to eat whatever I wanted was, and still is, wonderful. Gaining the weight also removed an obstacle to intimacy with Dan. I knew that looking so thin that he questioned if I were fully recovered would have left him feeling uneasy about growing close to me.

Dan and I dated for two years and fell in love with each other. One warm, late, summer evening, on a Labor Day weekend to the Washington coast, we went to the beach and sat on the rocks watching the sunset. The sun was like a huge firey ball sitting on top of the ocean. We watched it slowly sink down below the horizon, leaving streaks of red and orange in the sky, and as the light was beginning to fade, Dan asked me to marry him. I felt like the warm glow of the sunshine had found a place in my heart. We were married three months later.

The challenges I faced when recovering from my eating disorder were great, but the only person with whom I had to interact was myself. The challenges I faced in my marriage had a second dimension, namely, the thoughts, feelings, and issues of another person whom I could not, despite my best efforts, control. This, in some ways, made them greater and more complex.

When I entered marriage, I was loving, yet afraid of becoming really close to another person. This fear manifested itself in ways that I did not understand, such as attempting to control Dan's weight and eating patterns, reacting with fear when he wanted to do things without me, and desperately trying to convince him of my point of view when we argued. I was afraid of anger or disapproval and sometimes responded to him as though he were my enemy rather than my spouse. It seemed as though my self-confidence was beginning to melt away into the relationship.

At first, I blamed him for our problems. I had worked so hard on my recovery that I could not imagine that there was any work left for me to do. My defensiveness and anger hurt him and pushed him away. At those times, my reactions felt uncontrollable, just like the eating disorder behaviors once did. I was reacting to Dan in the same way I had reacted as a child when my father made what felt to me like a critical comment—namely, an odd combination of lashing out in anger followed by a desperate attempt to please to make everything okay. This did not help my relationship with my father, nor did it help my relationship with Dan.

My reactions were so deeply ingrained that I was not consciously aware of what I was doing. I decided to seek therapy because I wanted an objective person to guide me. Already a psychologist at the time, I felt a little apprehensive about asking for help, because it meant admitting to a colleague that I was not perfect. I did it anyway, though, allowing myself to benefit from the same kind of guidance, focused attention, and caring that I extend to my patients. It felt really good.

In therapy, I discovered a whole new layer of issues and experienced an even deeper level of healing inside. My therapist gave me a new way to think about my interactions. As she explained her perspective, I was able to become more objective and realistic without taking everything personally. Changing how I responded to and interpreted what happened in our relationship affected how Dan reacted to me, and our intimacy deepened.

For instance, I learned that I reacted defensively most often when afraid that he would leave me if my weaknesses and imperfections were exposed. I realized that this fear was primarily a consequence of my difficulty in fully accepting myself, and not of Dan's feelings toward me. Because I often equated criticism with rejection, learning that being criticized can be an opportunity for personal growth and deepening of intimacy was tremendously freeing.

Also, I was surprised to find that when I encouraged Dan to express his emotions to me, I took everything so much to heart that my own reactions interfered with my ability to listen to his feelings. Becoming more detached from my feelings at those times has helped me be more supportive of him and to better understand his needs. Although I knew intellectually that listening to and validating his emotions instead of defending myself would build rather than destroy intimacy, it took a while for that concept to penetrate to an emotional level.

Although one may infer from what I have written that my relationship with Dan was beset with problems, all of which were due to my issues, the reality is that ours is a strong relationship with its share of happy and close times. He brought his own set of issues into the marriage, which he has worked on as well, but that is his story and not mine. We both desire the best possible relationship and are committed to working out difficult issues that are barriers to intimacy in order to make things even better between us. I will always be grateful to him for helping

her sitting on my bed before I went to sleep saying, "No smilees!" I would try as hard as I could not to smile, but my mouth would curl up at the corners and we would laugh and laugh. One day, my mother bought a little, gray, toy mouse for me (which I still have). He was holding a kernel of corn in his front paws, had a long, fuzzy tail, and "lived" in my dresser drawer. At bedtime, "he" came out of the drawer and "listened" to me say my prayers. After I said "Amen," the mouse would say, "Duh," even though he was fully instructed not to do so. Every night, I would say my prayers all the while anticipating what would happen. When I finished, my mother and I would laugh really hard after the inevitable "duh" was uttered. These little incidents became treasured moments for me as I connected with the inner child in my mother. Krisanna and I play these same games, and I feel a wonderful sense of closeness to her and my mother at the same time.

It has been while developing my relationship with Krisanna, however, that some of my most profound realizations about intimacy have occurred. I have seen that most of the time relating with a child is fun and easy. At other times, especially when I am feeling sad, tired, sick, or upset, it requires great perseverance to continue to be sensitive to my child's needs and to be gentle in my responses.

From the time she was born, I have been struck by Krisanna's desire to communicate strong emotions. She has shown me that the feelings I see many of my adult patients struggling to express in their intimate relationships are present from birth. It is as if the capacity for intimacy and desire to be close are always present, and will flourish or not depending on whether they are thwarted or supported by parents and other significant adults. I am acutely aware that my responses to Krisanna's feelings—encouraging their expression versus shutting her down—will have a tremendous impact on her relationships as she grows older.

In her book, *Your Child: From Birth to Age Five,* Penelope Leach wrote that a major reason for the two's being "terrible" is that children are experiencing emotions at a level of intensity that is new and frightening, and desperately need adults to teach them how to manage these feelings. If they are punished or rejected for expressing strong emotion, they will learn to defend against feelings, act them out, or express them indirectly—all of which create problems in intimate relationships as adults.

I thought about Dr. Leach's words one night when I was helping Krisanna get ready for bed. I was tired and so was she. She would not let me put her pajamas on and I got frustrated and left the room. She knew I was angry. She started to cry, and after a few minutes I calmed down, went back to her room, and picked her up, asking, "Why are you crying?" She replied, "I'm sad because I don't like you to be mad at me." My heart melted as I empathized with the feeling she expressed. I remember feeling exactly as she did many times when I was a child. Having no recollection of ever telling my parents that I felt that way, I was amazed at how clearly she expressed her emotions at such a young age.

Not only am I encouraging Krisanna to express her strong emotions, I am also encouraging her to express *all* of her emotions. One instance that comes to mind became an opportunity for me to teach her that anger is a normal part of a close relationship and that conflict is resolvable, concepts that I did not learn until I was recovering from my eating disorder.

"Krisanna, you cannot take off your seatbelt in the car because it is dangerous!" I said in a stern voice on the way home from a rather stressful trip to the local shopping mall.

"I'm mad!" my daughter exclaimed loudly, her little eyes flashing and her body tense with anger. She was two-and-a-half years old at the time and was already able to express feelings more clearly than I did at age twenty! Then, as if to underline and add boldface type to her words, she hit me on the arm.

"It is not okay to hit Mama! It is okay to be angry and say it, but it is not okay to hit. I'm mad, too, because I don't like it when you hit me." What I said was fine, but my voice had more of an edge to it than was necessary. We had had a difficult day and were both feeling irritable by this time.

We drove in silence for a few minutes. Then I felt a little hand touch my arm and she said, "I'm being gentle now." I held her hand and said, "Are you still mad?" She said, "No." I replied, "I'm not either," and we talked about what had happened. Afterward, I said, "Sometimes we get mad at each other, but then we can talk about it and it's okay, right?" She said, "Yeah."

I have wondered how different the relationship between Krisanna and I would be if I were still engaged in eating disorder behaviors. I doubt I could have given her the amount or quality of care I would have wanted to give as a parent or she would have needed as a child. While anorexic and bulimic, my attention was almost always divided—a part of me focused on the here and now, another part was obsessed with calorie counting, weight, food, and so on. I know there would have been times when I would have had to choose between engaging in my behaviors and caring for my child. Frankly, I do not know if I would have always made the right choice.

I also believe that the tension between us would have increased dramatically, because I would have had less available emotional and physical energy. Being frequently preoccupied with food and having unpredictable emotions based on my weight, what I had eaten, or my exercise regime, would have created distance between us and severely limited the potential for our developing a healthy, intimate, mother/daughter relationship.

Closing Thoughts

When I was a child, one of my favorite books was entitled *David and the Phoenix*. It is the story of a boy who befriended the phoenix, a bird of gorgeous plumage. The most memorable part for me was when the phoenix intuitively sensed its impending death and prepared its own funeral pyre, as a phoenix customarily does at the end of its 500 to 600 year lifespan. The bird then rose from the ashes of the fire with feathers of gold and a new, radiant beauty.

I think people who have recovered from eating disorders are like the phoenix. The recovery process is analogous to the funeral pyre, symbolizing both an ending, in this case of a very painful part of life, and a transformation. People who recover are like that golden bird. They have an inner beauty, a radiant strength, and a chosen path which has given them a new lease on life.

213

Recovering from my eating disorder is one of my greatest accomplishments. It was also a new beginning for me, opening doors that would otherwise have remained closed had I stayed anorexic or bulimic. Recovery did not take away life's problems or hurts, but it did make it possible for me to live life, with its odd mixture of pain and joy, to the utmost. I am now able to experience the highs and lows that come with intimate relationships, to share in the building of the most intimate of all relationships—marriage—and to participate fully in what has been for me one of the most awe-inspiring, humbling, wonderful experiences of life—developing a relationship with a child. I, like the phoenix, have been transformed.

One day, Krisanna and I were playing on the floor. While I was engrossed in making a cat out of felt for her, Krisanna suddenly came over and put her arms around my neck, gave me a big hug, then said, "I love you, Mama." I felt so warm inside. It was as though the sun was shining on my heart, a feeling similar to the one I felt when I became engaged to Dan. Moments like this one validate that the time and energy I spent recovering from my eating disorder were worthwhile. I am very grateful that I am able to share in the lives of my husband, child, and other family members without being haunted by the fear of being fat or the obsession with food and weight.

Avis Rumney

*E*diting an anthology is not an easy job. I have done it once before for a book entitled **Recoveries**, which also included a chapter by Avis Rumney, and I can remember vowing never to undertake such a project again. However, my vision for **Full Lives** blocked out the inevitable nightmare of coordinating many authors' work at the same time. The urge to bring these extraordinary women together in one volume and voice was overwhelming.

Avis was one of the first people I thought of for **Full Lives**, because working with her on the first book was an absolute delight. She has always been gentle, positive, and respectful towards me, and has often taken the time to share her life and support mine. We had one particularly sweet conversation during our collaboration on this book, when both of us had lost a loved-one within a few months of each other. I felt deeply that she understood what I was going through, and appreciated her willingness to connect with me. I imagine that with such qualities, as well as a voice like honey, she is a wonderful therapist! As a licensed Marriage, Family and Child Counselor in Northern California for over ten years, she has specialized in eating disorders, and wrote her first book, **Dying to Please: Anorexia and Its Cure**, about her personal journey and recovery process.

Avis was thirteen years old when she began a struggle with anorexia nervosa that lasted almost two decades. On the doorstep of womanhood, she had to face what all young girls face: physical maturation and the uncertainty of what it *means to be a woman. It is not surprising that she focused on her size and shape as the keys to her happiness, success, and femininity—dieting has become almost a right of passage for adolescent girls. Their role models and peers are all weight conscious, and they are relentlessly bombarded with media images of beautiful, thin women (many of them only girls themselves and some anorexic at that). What's more, changing one's body is one of the most (if not the most) widely publicized ways for a woman to "improve" herself. For this reason, when Avis resolved to lose weight, she was embarking on a serious quest for meaning in her life and an identity with which to feel secure.*

Unfortunately, society's great promise to women—that beauty has value and is therefore a means to a better life—is false and a diversion from other avenues to personal fulfillment. The quest for the perfect body is fraught with feelings of inadequacy, alienation, and disempowerment. Ironically, the very thing which is portrayed as important for women is that which makes makes them physically smaller, emotionally exhausted, and mentally preoccupied! In Avis' case, which is typical of many women, she was so busy creating an image that would conform to the opinions of others that she neglected her own needs, and became incapacitated with regards to decision making, and deaf to her inner voice.

Avis is a relentless seeker, however, and she finally entered therapy "hoping to learn the secret to human existence I had somehow never learned." With guidance and support, she faced the same questions she had faced at age thirteen: Who am I? What do I like? How do I make choices? This time, though, she did not look for the answers in the eyes of others or in the reflection of her mirror, but within her own self on a journey "Beyond the Looking Glass".

216

Beyond the Looking Glass

Avis Rumney

In the house where I grew up, one entire wall of the upstairs hallway was dominated by an eight-foot wide, floor-to-ceiling mirror. Each time I went from my bedroom to the stairs or walked up the stairs to my room, I passed the mirror, occasionally glancing sideways at my profile. For years, I took the mirror for granted. It was simply a part of the house, no more remarkable than the polished wooden bannister or the sunny alcove outside my bedroom.

Then I entered junior high school. How I looked suddenly became very important. Each morning, I would scrutinize my appearance before this giant glass. Did I look okay? Was my skirt the right length? What would the other kids say about me? Worse yet, what would they think?

One day after school, I announced proudly to my mother that I'd eaten three desserts at lunch. She looked at me with consternation and replied, "You're getting fat!" I was crushed. I had expected praise! Fat sounded like a truly horrible fate. Soon after her pronouncement, I looked hard at myself in the hall mirror. It was true. I was fat and fat was me.

I had to lose weight. I had to show my mother she was wrong. Was this how everyone saw me? As fat? As inadequate? I had to prove that I was okay. I started to diet . . . furtively, secretly. I subsisted on fruit, throwing away all but my apple at lunch. I devoured oranges in my bedroom after school and smuggled my dinner from the table to the garbage pail in my napkin. I embarked on a painful, tortured struggle with food, my body, and my self. Hourly, I stood before that hall mirror, turning every direction and peering at my reflection. Were the bulges disappearing? Was I thin enough yet?

I became anorexic, although I didn't know it at the time and would not have admitted it anyway. I lived in a constant state of inner turmoil. I was a frightened, immature almost-person, who was never good enough and was desperate to accomplish *something* that would affirm my right to exist. I was forever grasping for an "it" outside of me that would make me feel whole inside. I continually compared myself to others, and to the person I thought I was supposed to be. Figuring out how I *should* be was a never-ending pursuit.

All around me were people who seemed to possess some secret about life that eluded me. My single wish was to acquire that self-confidence. If I could just get thin enough, wouldn't the emptiness disappear, filled with the success of my achievement? Before I had a chance to find out, my parents and family doctor intervened with the threat of hospitalization. I had to maintain a healthy weight to keep them at bay. Outside, I remained a "normal" weight. Inside, I felt emptiness and despair.

Blind Spots

I was sixteen when I went away to college. I felt even younger, and very naive. My eighteen-year-old freshman roommate was a bouncy girl with a broad smile and big breasts who had been dating since she was eleven. Her pudginess didn't seem to bother her; my barely pinchable flesh tormented me.

My roommate spent her evenings partying; I spent mine alternately studying and crying. I went to my professors for help and reassurance, convinced that I was going to flunk out, although I rarely received a grade below C. They told me how well I was doing, but I still felt wretched. If I was doing so well, how come I felt so miserable? If grades were important and I was getting good ones, why did I feel such anguish? My roommate seemed content with straight D's. I was convinced that success in college was directly proportional to breast size and inversely related to brain use. Being both flat-chested and obsessed with studying, I was a failure.

I dropped out of college after three semesters and moved to New York City to find a job. I was eighteen and very discouraged. No longer under parental supervision and earning barely enough money to buy food, my weight began to drop again. Each day at lunchtime I bought one sandwich from the corner deli—egg salad and bacon on whole wheat toast with lettuce and mayonnaise. I ate little else. Hungry and despondent, I both feared and felt a peculiar kinship with the Bowery bums I passed in the gutters near my lower East Side flat. As I scurried through the bustling streets of New York and boarded the subway, bumping elbows with hundreds of seemingly self-assured and goal-directed individuals, I felt lost and empty. I encountered people of various ages, cultural backgrounds and economic situations, some of them clearly less fortunate than I. Nonetheless, I was certain every one of them was privy to a personal peace I lacked.

I decided that maybe college was the answer after all. I returned to school with family support and struggled for two and a half years to get a bachelor's degree. None of my schoolwork seemed good enough, though, no matter what my grades or my weight. To my surprise and chagrin, I was awarded honors, but the accolades only magnified the emptiness inside. I was plagued by the conviction that I didn't deserve recognition. Since the age of twelve, I tried to prove I was as good as other people, but now with awards demonstrating my scholastic success, I felt like an impostor. Inside I was hollow; outside I was thin. Neither thinness nor success brought me satisfaction.

I concluded that a good job—with my hard-earned B.A. a prerequisite—would give me an inner sense of self. As the scientific assistant to the head curator in the fish department at the Museum of Natural History in New York, I fiercely dedicated my attention to the tasks my supervisor assigned to me. I was determined to do my best. Despite his praise for my efficiency, though, I knew he secretly expected more.

Fueled by fear, I zipped from project to project in a frenzy of productivity. When I walked down the museum hall, I'd suck in my stomach and walk erectly, hoping anyone who saw me would perceive strength and competence in my thin, taut body and ramrod-like carriage. When the department members gathered for tea and cookies each afternoon, I hovered nervously at the periphery of the circle, feeling awkward and out-of-place as the others chatted casually. When they munched nonchalantly on sugary sweets, I obsessed over whether I could permit myself to eat even *one* cookie, and if so, *which one?*

The department members, from middle-aged curators with doctorate degrees to the high-school educated clerk and technician, bantered lightly as I clenched my teacup. I hoped desperately that no one would ask me anything which might expose my ignorance. How was it that each person in this mixed gathering possessed a confidence I so glaringly lacked? How could they be so comfortable when I was so ill at ease?

I pursued each new direction with the hope that it would bring me inner peace, but marriage, graduate school, teaching assistantships, and even a retreat to Cape Cod to hand-paint t-shirts for tourists left me with the same disquiet. Outside I was thin, although I knew I wasn't thin enough; because, if I were thin enough, surely I'd be happy! Where was contentment to be found? I needed help to answer this.

Looking for Help

Finally, I entered therapy, hoping to learn the key to life—the secret that gave meaning to human existence that I had somehow never learned. How had I managed to be out of the room when that gem was bestowed?

In therapy I discovered that there was no secret key! Although each nugget of information seemed to add another piece that helped make my life work better, none of them alone supplied the magical missing element I

possessed the makings of an identity that didn't depend on my body size. There was something *inside* of me to go by!

Making Decisions for Myself

Not being sure of my likes and dislikes rendered making even simple decisions an ordeal. Whenever I could, I would let other people decide for me. I didn't trust myself to look within or think I had anything within to look to! I'd ask my friends, colleagues, boyfriend, and therapist, "What should I do about...?" and usually they would tell me. Some would reply, "You ought to..." Others would say, "If I were you, I would..." And still others would inquire, "What do *you* want to do?"

The last response never failed to throw me. To it I'd reply despairingly that I didn't *know* what I wanted, and wish that the answer would drop out of the sky and into my mind.

I was convinced that there were two choices, "right" and "wrong," and my job was to unravel the puzzle and figure out which was which. This seemed to demand some foresight which I lacked. How could I know what would work out to be right?

I was sometimes able to figure out what I *didn't* want, even if I didn't have a clue about what I *did* want. Occasionally, by eliminating choices that didn't feel right, I'd arrive by approximations at an answer, but once again this made me feel inadequate. Why was finding an answer so arduous a process for me but not for others? I suspected that my quest for the perfect answer played a part.

I came to see that rarely was there only one *right* answer. Some answers fit better at some times than others, and different answers were appropriate for different people. The difficult part was trusting that I had some cues inside to know whether something was right for me. Even more threatening was learning to look to myself first and depend on an intuitive "that feels right" experience, before I considered other people's opinions. I needed to set aside my expectations of how *I should know* and stay with my conflicting voices and uncertainty long enough to *let myself know*.

It was scary for me to rely on such an imprecise method. The process was often the same—questioning whether I would find an answer I could trust, groping around outside of me for clues, then turning to my own thoughts and feelings for hints. I would hear a cacophony of inner voices—wishes, judgments, strategies, and "what if's." Finally, from some intuitive place, that I couldn't locate anatomically, would emanate the answer that I had doubted I would ever find. It was ironic that the very body I spurned possessed the answers I so desperately sought.

After I made a decision, I discovered both relief and gratification in dismissing the alternatives. I would tell myself firmly, "This is what I've decided. I've made the best decision I can under the present circumstances. Changing my mind will only make me feel worse." Letting go took practice. My tendency was to question myself relentlessly so as to avoid making mistakes or experiencing regrets. Only by consciously focusing on my final decision was I able to stop obsessing about my other choices—but what an improvement over staying stuck in murky indecision!

It was this very process that I needed to accept as my own, no matter what worked for other people. It certainly wasn't the method I would have chosen! Yet each time I muddled through this way, it renewed my faith that I really did have answers.

I hoped that making decisions would get simpler and less painful with practice. My life was full of countless choices—big and small, professional and personal, whether to go to a workshop, do a project with a colleague, rent an office, do committee work, take an afternoon off, hold a baby shower for a pregnant friend, buy her a gift, change my hairstyle—the list was endless. But I realized if I didn't expect making decisions to be easy, and simply accepted that they were going to be tough and uncomfortable for me, then I wouldn't feel so bad about myself in the process. I needed to keep reminding myself that few decisions were immutable, none were perfect, and all had consequences.

Farewell to Perfectionism: I Am Not What I Do

It seemed that I was making progress. I was getting better at expressing opinions and making decisions, but my self-worth still depended on my accomplishments—not, as in my anorexic days, on how little I could eat or weigh, but on how much I could get done. I was oppressed by "doingness." Shelves were dusted, plants watered, papers stacked, and lists checked off, but it didn't fill the emptiness inside.

If I noticed something that needed to be done, I was filled with anxiety until it was finished. As soon as this task was completed, I'd get caught up in executing the next one. Inside, I felt like a racecar going at high speed around a track, in constant motion but never getting closer to the finish line. What kept me from stopping and being content with what I had already done, or even with not doing anything at all? This was the same quest for accomplishment that I'd felt all my life. Whether my present focus was on pounds lost, grades received, or projects completed, the proclamation was the same: If it wasn't perfect, it wasn't good enough.

Last summer, I spent many hours clearing a big plot of shoulder-high weeds in my backyard. With long-handled clippers, I levelled thick-stalked weeds and pulled up the roots. I raked up the weeds along with masses of dead branches and leaves that had fallen over the years. Once I'd cleared the area, I carried in nine hundred pounds of black pebbles and painstakingly spread them out to form a path. With rocks that I had gathered, I outlined a couple of islands of earth. I sprinkled the islands heavily with wood chips and then arranged on them sturdy clay pots, which I planted with large ornamental shrubs.

Later, however, when I looked out in the back, what I saw was not the decoratively landscaped area with carefully pruned plants and pebbles raked free of debris. Instead, my eyes focussed on a bare stretch of worn fence and the dilapidated deck bereft of greenery that was *next* to the garden I had constructed.

My glance was not simply a fleeting observation of a project I had yet to tackle, but a source of anguish. I could not enjoy the garden I had created because of the ugliness I had left beside it! My eyes were inexorably drawn to this worn fence. It was a symbol of my emphasizing negative rather than positive that had haunted me all my life, and the very thing that continued to undermine my self-esteem. Nothing was ever good enough because it was never perfect. And while my impulse was to rush over and fill that untended area, I knew that this would not solve the inner problem.

The force that riveted my eyes to this barren place each time I looked out into the yard (or even pictured it in my mind) was the same tyrant that had always compelled me to do more and never allowed me peace. I had let this insatiable demon run my life for far too many years! I had to find a way to turn off this inner oppressor.

One afternoon when I was standing in my back yard, I let my gaze move from the manicured garden back to the old, worn fence. This time, I wouldn't allow myself to move away or make plans about how to "fix" it. I stood there, rooted to the ground, determined to overcome my negativity. It didn't feel good, but as I stayed, the anxiety diminished. I felt a heaviness, a sense of loss and depression, but I also felt calm. I *could* stand it! Perhaps this was acceptance. The project wasn't finished, many projects weren't, but I could stand it. They weren't reflections of me, or even if they were, so be it. I wasn't perfect, either, and no amount of activity was going to make me so.

Accepting Who I Am

Even if I could voice some likes and dislikes, make choices—sometimes imperfect ones—and stick to them, could I really *accept* the choices I was making? Many times I didn't really want to own them. I preferred to push away that responsibility and pretend that things just worked out a certain way. Over and over again, I came back to the question of *how could I really trust myself?*

This was an enigma. It seemed that I would need to be more accepting of myself in order to trust myself, but how could I accept myself if I didn't feel worthy of self-acceptance?

Several years ago, I asked a therapist whether self-esteem came from inside or from outside. She replied that self-esteem came from those around you reflecting your own goodness. In other words, kids develop self-esteem in the process of growing up as their parents and others around them value them for who they are. But what about people who had missed those crucial interactions? Could self-esteem really be developed at a later age? While the purpose of therapy, especially of reparenting, seemed to be for the client to internalize a healthy experience that was missed or skewed earlier, was it really possible to make up for the enormity of the earlier deficit? Therapy clearly helped this process, but what else needed to be there? What did the client need to provide? Wouldn't there always be a scar that new learning would never erase? I didn't know if I would find the answers to all of these questions, but I knew I had to find out what, for me, would improve my self-esteem.

I knew that my therapists, friends, and colleagues had all been instrumental in providing new mirroring which had helped me develop a healthier sense of myself. But I also believed that I had more work to do and some other pieces to fit in place. I still didn't have a consistent inner sense of, "I am a worthy person just for being who I am."

It seemed impossible to own those things about myself which for years I had disdained. But when I did, I felt an inner solidness and a peace. Covering up what I didn't like about myself, or trying to be who I wasn't by becoming unnaturally thin or aspiring to superhuman perfection, perpetuated the very emptiness I sought to fill! It seemed

However, when we finally met in person after almost a decade of letters and phone calls, these things weren't the only foundation for the friendship that blossomed. In fact, our initial conversations were somewhat like looking in a mirror! We immediately sensed that we could learn a lot from each other. I remember one particularly fun and intense discussion, at a conference where we were both speakers, that began over dessert and ended in the early morning hours.

*I have placed Jane's chapter deep in the heart of this book, because it is about a subject which is close to the heart of every **Full Lives** author. Jane writes about her connection with the Self, a theme that has appeared over and over in other stories. Joan Ebbitt refers to "that wonder of spirit within and outside of me." Susan Kano puts her faith in "an inner realm of wisdom." Avis Rumney writes, "I had held the key to life all along and it was me." Eileen T. Bills ends her story with "I am left with me, and that is finally a secure and comforting experience."*

In the course of their healing journeys, every one of these women discovered that their preoccupation with the hungers of the body kept them from acknowledging and satisfying the hungers of their souls. When they turned their attention inward, though, in search of what Jane calls "a place of vision, no matter how tiny," they found within themselves a source of meaning, creativity, love, power, and unlimited possibilities for their lives. Jane invites us to investigate this "realm of miracles" for it exists within each of us and is the key to living a full life.

Jane E. Latimer is a visionary and a poet, with remarkable powers of self-inquiry, creativity and expression. With great respect for the path she has chosen, I introduce "Visions".

Visions

Jane E. Latimer

I wake up. It is the middle of the night. It is dark and the house is quiet. Depressed, and in a cold sweat, I touch my thighs and stomach. They feel too big. I feel sick. I did it again last night after dinner. I hate myself. Why can't I stop?

Quietly, I slip out of bed in the dark. Moving slowly, careful not to wake my sister, careful not to make a sound, I grope my way down the hall, using my hands to guide the way. I know this path by heart. I've done this many times before.

I hear a sound in the bathroom. One of my parents is awake. I wait, my heart beating. I must be sure they don't suspect I'm here. The toilet flushes and then the house is quiet again. I wait. Cautiously, I approach the kitchen and close the door. Now I can relax. The light from the refrigerator illuminates the room. My hand reaches for the freezer. I pop a couple of pieces of frozen bread into the toaster. My fingers grab a gob of of vanilla ice cream. When the toast is ready, I spread it with cream cheese *and pop two more frozen pieces of bread into the toaster. Grabbing a handful of fig newtons, still munching on the toast, some part of me realizes what I'm doing. The tears begin to run down my cheeks. Why can't I stop? My head hurts . . . mouth still full of cookies . . . I'm aware of my hand reaching for the leftover meatloaf. I grab some meat . . . can't take the time to cut it . . . can't stop . . . toast, cheese, cookies, peanut butter . . . stomach about to burst, and my eyes are wet with tears. My heart explodes with pain; my lungs are tight; I have a hard time breathing. Grabbing a handful of graham crackers, I make my way painfully, slowly, back to my bed.**

(Jane, age seventeen)

Little did I know at that age that I would struggle another ten years before making any attempt to get real help, that my recovery would then take another three to five years, or that my career would eventually involve helping others find freedom from food and weight issues.

Twenty-seven years later, I now understand what I could not then—that emotional eating has a purpose. It enables the individual to avoid issues that would be impossible to face head-on. In my case (as is true for many), there was no avenue through which to channel all the feelings stirred up in adolescence. There was no vocabulary through which to express those feelings and

---

* Jane E. Latimer, *Living Binge-Free*, Denver, LivingQuest, 1988.

no support for the expression of them, because my parents had no way to deal with adolescent changes around identity and sexuality.

For the adolescent, these issues run something like: "Who am I if I'm not my parents' child? Who am I in my own right? Who am I as a sexual being? How do I juggle new desires within the old context?" Just as the Self is emerging, so is the body emerging in a new way. With no understanding of the changes that are taking place, there is confusion, unrest, and depression.

Emotional eating takes up time, space, and energy. It fills an emptiness, a longing, and guards against fears of powerlessness, loss of control, and intimacy. Emotional eating represents not a hunger for food, but for physical, emotional, and spiritual connectedness to Self, to others, and to the world.

It follows, then, that one's disordered eating can be used to point the way towards an authentic identity and sexuality. If one understands that recovery entails not trying to get rid of a problem, but rather journeying through it, the eating behavior may be used as a key. With it, one can open a doorway and enter into the inner chamber of one's true Self. In this way, the behavior itself can be a guide to the anxieties, fears, and other discomforts that underlie it. With support, one may come to understand these discomforts, for they correspond to injuries that have occurred along the developmental path. These injuries represent missing pieces of a puzzle which, when completed, form the Self.

My greatest gratitude is to have been given the opportunity to discover and put my puzzle together. I have come to know without a shadow of a doubt the miracle we call transformation. I've been blessed by this experience. Without my eating disorder, I would not have known where to look or which direction to journey.

It is always possible to begin anew.

I have had two rebirths, led three separate lives. My first life was that of a bulimic, and in that life I felt powerless, empty, and despairing. My second brought freedom from food issues, yet was still bound by emptiness and despair. In my third, the one I am now living, I have opened to new levels of joy and creativity and an increased ability to master my life—to realize my dreams and my goals. It feels as if the spiritual energy that runs through me is rooted in the earth, and with this rootedness I am able to support, through my physical body, those things that come from the world of dreams and spirit. The merging of the spiritual energy with the physical body has been my greatest joy.

Individuals who are struggling with emotional eating must learn to experience themselves through the body. The body is the vehicle through which our true Self expresses. If we are split off from the body, the true Self has nowhere to go.

Imagine a glass of water. The glass represents the physical vehicle in which the water, or energy of the individual, is contained. If you take away the glass, there is no container. Most emotional eaters do not have a physical container because for whatever reason, whether it be from trauma or an abusive or neglectful childhood environment, they have chosen to leave their body. To stay in the body would be to feel too much pain. Imagine an individual walking around without a physical container to hold his or her energy. It would be like removing the glass. The water would spill out in all directions. If the water—our personal energy—doesn't stay together as a unit, it becomes impossible for us to function.

In order for the out-of-body individual to function, a makeshift container must be fabricated. We do this in many different ways. The most obvious way is to attach to outside objects to find self-definition. A person may cling to other people, food, rules, behaviors, or ideas to create an identity.

To find one's true Self, one must be willing to let go of the makeshift container while learning to re-occupy the physical container, which is the body. (There is, without a doubt, a clear experiential difference between being in and out of the body. When I help people to come into the body—to feel the flow of their energetic Self through their body—there is no mistaking the sense of fullness.)

Once we are present in our bodies, we are forced to look around and notice what we have created for ourselves in our real physical lives. That means we no longer live through the fantasies, expectations, or ideas we have had. Rather, we live in the reality of the physical present. This can be painful if what we see is unpleasant—unfriendly environments, relationships, work situations, disease—but with awareness can come change. Full living—to be truly filled—is to feel an absolutely tangible energy moving from head to toe, to experience that our reality is of our making and to know that we can change it.

The emptiness that once ruled my life has fallen away and I am gifted with the experience of miracles.

I sit on my front steps, my heart aching. I look at a tree that sits in my front yard. I sketch its outline with my eyes. As I do, I move into the center of that tree. I feel its life, its glory. I never saw that tree before. It's beautiful with its cracked branches, not a perfect tree, not the kind of tree you'd notice in passing and say, "What a magnificent tree." Just a very plain tree and yet as I look, it opens itself to me and reveals its soul to me and says, "I am a glorious tree, a being of grandeur. Thank you for taking the time to see me for who I am." *
(Jane, age thirty-three)

Growth is about belief and how one sees oneself in relationship to oneself, to others, and to the world at large. Our beliefs are imprinted into the physical, emotional, and energetic aspects of each one of us. They stifle, overlay, and block our fruition. To heal, it is necessary to bring awareness to these imprints so that they may be peeled off one layer at a time, like an onion. As this is accomplished, there is an incredible flourishing—spurts of growth, hope, enthusiasm for the creative possibilities of one's life.

As we understand and look with new awareness at those factors which have limited us, we are free to make new choices in our life. Because we are creative, spiritual beings, the choices are unlimited. As we peel off the layers of our tightly-held belief systems, we are free to transform our self-image, our character style, and our

---

* Latimer, op. cit., p. 10.

cognitive and behavioral patterns. We are reborn. As we connect with the creative, spiritual being that lives within, we come home to our Self.

Vision is at the heart of creative living. Humanity is unique in its ability to see further than what has already been actualized. We strive to make our lives better. Hope feeds vision, for embedded within our desires is the hope that what we desire can be. Desire is a powerful motivating force. Desire cannot live without hope. It is our ability to imagine what might be, combined with our hopes and desires, that channels our creative powers.

Thus, the desire to live free of emotional eating and the hope that it is possible, combined with imagination, create a vision. This powerful force enables us to then look for the inspiration, support, and tools to make what we envision real.

Each and every one of us must connect to a place of vision, no matter how tiny. We are not to think that what we envision is not possible. That may be the case, but that is not our decision. That is God's. Our only job is to connect to the vision and move steadfastly forward, putting one foot slowly in front of the other, always attuned to the subtle nuances and changes that can happen.

My healing vision began as I was in the throes of a dark and miserable life, coming in the form of a profound desire and hope that someday I would be free. It has taken me to that place and beyond. The vision grew as I grew, in increments. Under its impetus, I marshalled all of my resources, all of my energy and focus, to attain my original goal—freedom from emotional eating. Eventually, after much effort and surrender, food ceased being an issue for me. That accomplished, I then dreamed of writing a book that would inspire people to heal. I accomplished that and my vision grew. I longed for direct one-on-one interaction with those who were struggling. That vision was accomplished and it grew further.

I am presently in a long-term process of co-creating a healing center which celebrates life and facilitates wholeness. I see adults and children together learning how to live in harmony and mutual respect, where families can learn the skills needed to raise a new generation of people capable of living cooperatively, responsibly, and creatively. I see a school whose purpose is to teach children to become citizens of the earth, to relate with awe to the unfoldment of life, to live in creative union with all other living beings. I see a healing environment in which people are shown how to live in spiritual, emotional, and physiological balance.

There is no greater pleasure than the experience of manifestation—that of having a vision (no matter how small) and seeing that vision become real. That is perhaps the greatest experience one can hope for, because it places one in the center of one's own divinity. It is also quite humbling, for the very act of creation is a mystery and lies within the realm of miracles. I am brought to my knees in gratitude for the gifts of healing and creative living that have been bestowed upon me.

Deep inside even the darkest of us, an ember glows. A spark remains. Ignite the ember with light of vision and feel a passion to create. Use creative energy and burst prior limitations—old concepts, core-beliefs, and life-perceptions. Anything is possible. Lose your self. Swim in the unfamiliar waters of universal energy and wonder, "Who am I?" The concepts that have kept us safe, but half-dead, are blown away and in their place is born a new self. In the mind a war rages—we want to stay on familiar land, yet we push onward beyond our limits. Walking forward into unknown territory, we are in awe of the universe that only once existed in our mind, faint and far away—as an idea, a dream, a vision.

> *You who know the mind-altering power of food know only a shadow of your true creative Self. You are thirsty for it and yet you know not where to find it. Perhaps recovery seems like death, for it promises no replacement for that passion. But I tell you: follow your dream and seek a teacher who can guide you inward to your spark. Ignite its power so you can live outside the death-like limitations of your compulsive self—living, breathing a part of the universal circle of dreams. For what you believe is who you are. Our world is nothing more than the manifestation of ideas that once lived inside our minds. What else is there, but to be part of this awesome circle of dreams made manifest, to be a player in and observe the universal creative laws at work within us?*
> *(Jane, age forty-four)*

Geneen Roth

*We have come full circle at the **Full Lives** dinner table, and Geneen Roth is seated to my immediate left. Actually, the conversation which follows is taken from several we have had as we have become friends over the past three years.*

*When I originally approached Geneen with the idea of contributing a chapter, we knew about each other but had never met. I had read her first book, **Feeding the Hungry Heart**, when it was published in 1982, and she had heard of me through a close mutual friend. She was in the midst of a writing project at the time, and was understandably hesitant. All four of Geneen's books are bestsellers, and she is in constant demand. The overwhelming success of her most recent book, **When Food is Love**, has made her time all the more precious, so she suggested we get acquainted and take it from there.*

We finally met in person when I picked her up at the airport in San Diego, where she was scheduled to give a weekend workshop. She was the last to get off the plane, smiling widely. We drove to a hotel nearby and spent a couple of hours in her room talking. Our discussion took on an immediate level of intimacy, which was quite wonderful and took me by surprise. We covered a wide range of topics, including our thoughts about love, spiritual life, women and food issues, and cats. We discovered that we have a lot in common, not the least of which is our devotion to our fat, white cats! (People tease her about Blanche, with lines like, "Have you thought about leading cat compulsive eating groups?")

*I was thrilled when Geneen agreed to contribute. Over the next three years, we spoke on the phone several times, and met for lunch near my home and for tea at hers. The chapter which follows is taken from those meetings, and I have chosen it as a conclusion to **Full Lives** for good reason—Geneen's words are an invitation for readers to take action. We cannot wait until we think we are thin enough, or good enough, or even recovered enough to begin living fully. We must stop judging ourselves so harshly. We are enough exactly as we are, as Geneen says, "an unrepeatable gift." What's more, giving of ourselves to the world can be healing, both personally and globally. She writes, "Each life matters. Each choice matters."*

Geneen is an extraordinary teacher who has touched many lives with her courage, honesty, and willingness to be open hearted. Her chapter, "Dessert", is a sweet to savor at the end of this delicious meal. I hope it inspires you to recognize and treasure your own inner sweetness. With sincere gratitude for her contribution and appreciation for her friendship, I introduce Geneen Roth.

Dessert

Geneen Roth

LINDSEY: For me, getting to know the *Full Lives* authors
so intimately has been the biggest reward of
putting this book together. You and I have been
in contact for almost three years, with short vis-
its and phone calls, and I have thoroughly enjoyed every conversation. After all of your personal work, writing, workshops, and television
appearances, do the issues of food and weight
affect you now?

GENEEN: I am flying to New York in a few weeks for my
father's seventieth birthday. My cousin, Anna,
and my mother and aunts will be there. For two
days after I found out that the women's
contingent was going to be at the party, I felt fat
and ugly, wondering how I could lose ten
pounds in two weeks. I ate when I wasn't hungry, I ate what I didn't want, and I ate to quiet
the relentless voice of "I'm not good enough."
When I realized what was going on, that I felt as
if I was seven years old again, about to parade
before the women in my family and hear their
comments on my body, I stopped dead in my

tracks. I thought, "Geneen, you've been working on this for fifteen years, and if you need to hear me say it again, I will: 'You're not fat and you're not ugly, and if your cousin Anna thinks your thighs are too big, that's her problem. It always was. Can we go back to being a grown-up now?'"

The issue is still alive for me. My weight doesn't vacillate anymore, and I don't go on binges. Now, it's the moment to moment awareness of how I treat myself, how I talk to myself, what it feels like to have a woman's body in a culture that objectifies women's bodies.

LINDSEY: I know what you mean. I've worked very hard to feel strong within myself and comfortable in my body, but I still live in a culture that glorifies thinness. Messages about women's bodies, some subtle and some not, are everywhere.

GENEEN: I open the pages of fashion magazines and see that the Twiggy look has made a comeback, that models who look like adolescent boys are parading as women, and that this is how beauty is being defined *again*. It's been thirty years since Twiggy appeared, and we're still wanting to strip women of their sumptuousness, their weightiness, their curves, their flesh, anything that reminds us of their gorgeous bodies and the power that resides with us—in us.

Fifty percent of all women are dieting at any moment and thirty-six billion dollars is spent on dieting and weight loss products every year. We're all trying to look like someone other than who we are.

The most insidious aspect of this epidemic, though, is that people don't consider dieting and weight loss as the problem; they think of them as the solution. Thinness is so valued by our culture that prejudice against fat people is acceptable. We all believe that being leggy and boney is better than being round and lush, and we all believe that if only we tried hard enough, we could be thin.

LINDSEY: But we don't *all* buy into it anymore. The women in this book have worked hard to be free from problems with food and weight. *And* they are speaking out. I think most of us who work in this field do so because we passionately want others to learn that there is a life beyond scales and a perfect body—a full life. Isn't that the work that you do?

GENEEN: My work as a teacher is about helping people see that we use food for emotional reasons. We use it to speak for us, to say things we feel we are not allowed to say directly. This is a shock to many women who think they eat when they are not hungry because they are spineless and lack willpower.

LINDSEY: They blame the fact that they can't get thin on themselves, but it's dieting that doesn't work!

GENEEN: Diets don't work—they never have and they never will. Given the chance and the opportunity to tell the truth about our experience of dieting, every woman would say that diets lead to an extraordinary amount of mistrust and pain, making us feel like hungry ghosts who can never get enough. If diets worked, we wouldn't have a thriving thirty-six-billion-dollar-a-year industry.

The only thing that will ever work is respecting the natural hungers of the body, treating ourselves with honor and respect, and learning to use our mouths to speak the truth as well as to eat the food.

LINDSEY: Certainly this would be easier if the culture felt safer and more satisfying to women.

GENEEN: True. I went to a lecture recently where the speaker said that "the culture is the family's family." When we talk about the obsession with food, we must also talk about our cultural obsession with the size of women's bodies, and what that obsession does to their minds and hearts. It is almost impossible to be a woman in this culture and feel powerful and gorgeous unless you have no thighs, no belly, no breasts—unless you don't look like a woman.

An impossible ideal is set up for us that we can never attain and the result is frustration, sorrow, and self-hatred. We could all work very hard on abuse that is family related, we could spend years in therapy, we could feel healthy and strong, but we still have to live in a culture that demeans the very essence of who we are. We need to be aware of how crazy the culture is and that it plays an essential role in how we feel about ourselves—as essential as the part our parents, teachers, or siblings play.

LINDSEY: But if the status of women in our culture remains the same, then why get better? Why go through the process of healing?

GENEEN: The purpose of healing is to go through the pain of the past, and then to actually live in the present: to be alive, to be present for a peony opening, or the color blue. And then we must take it one more step. Take all this aliveness, allow yourself to feel what is going on around you, and act on what you see, what you feel. Take that healing and move out into the world with it to make the contribution that only you, as the unrepeatable gifted being that you are, can make.

My teacher, Thich Nhat Hahn, a Vietnamese Zen master, talks about "engaged Buddhism"—getting off your cushion and taking all that mindfulness, that generosity of spirit, that huge heart into our damaged, beautiful, fragile world.

LINDSEY: I've tried to do that in my own life, and it takes courage. Expressing yourself is risky, but I've found that when I approach a task with an open heart, good things happen.

GENEEN: I used to think that I needed to be healed in order to work in the world, and now I see that I was looking at it in a skewed way. One adds to the other. Working in the world, doing what you love, heals you. And the more you value yourself, the more aware you become, the more energy you have to work in the world.

I think many people are waiting to feel healed before they work at something they love, or before they speak out about things they feel are unjust. They don't feel they have the right to do it, and they think that when they are "healed," or thin, they will have the energy. But it doesn't work that way. We can begin now, today, exactly where we are.

My recent work is focusing more on taking the energy that we wrap up in food and using it to act in the world. The more women are centered on trying to be impossibly thin, the less energy they will have to speak out about other issues. Although it seems as if the dominant culture is terribly threatened by the natural creativity and lushness of women's bodies, the real threat will be when more women speak out about their visions. Half the race in our culture has been gagged by the terrible obsession with thinness.

LINDSEY: I know that you have been speaking out lately.

GENEEN: Yes, I have. In working with my friend and teacher, Joanna Macy, I've become fascinated with the connection between what women are doing to their bodies, and what is being done to the earth. The drive for control, power, domination, the need to win, and to possess is how we have almost destroyed the earth. It is also how we've been destroying our bodies.

Every day, forty thousand children under the age of five die of malnutrition, we lose fifty plant and animal species, and seventy-five thousand acres of virgin rainforest are destroyed. Most of us are walking around in a lot of pain because of what we see happening to the earth, and yet we feel completely overwhelmed. There seems to be nothing we can do about it. We won't let ourselves feel that pain, so we hold fast to the magical belief that if only we were thin, everything would be all right.

LINDSEY: If thinness is the solution, then food and weight are the enemies! But many of the women in this book have said that facing these issues—these "enemies"—has been one of the most significant and rewarding experiences of their lives.

GENEEN: When we make friends with food and what it means to us—the role it plays in our emotional life—we are freed to be our authentic selves and to give what is only ours to give. I receive letters from women in their seventies and eighties who are still struggling with trying to be thinner. They have spent their lives the way we are spending our lives—with the insane belief that looking the way the people on Madison Avenue think we should look will actually give us peace, a measure of happiness, the feeling that we have done something worthy with our lives.

A writer named Annie Dillard said, "How we spend our days is how we spend our lives." The thousands of daily choices we make through the years are strung together to make a life. Each life matters, each choice matters. And so, the question is, what are you going to do with this wild, precious life of yours?

About
the
Authors

Eileen T. Bills

Eileen T. Bills received her bachelor's degree from the University of California at Los Angeles, and her Ph.D. in counseling psychology from the University of Houston. Her interest in the area of eating disorders influenced her to write both her Masters thesis and Ph.D. dissertations about this subject. She has authored and presented numerous research papers on related topics, has worked with women with eating disorders on an inpatient hospital unit, and has treated adolescents and women with eating disorders both individually and in groups. She is presently involved in researching sexual abuse precursors to eating disorders and resultant psychopathology.

Eileen has been married for twelve years and has four children. To her, this is the most important aspect of her life because she is now able to "really experience loving and living."

Joan Ebbitt

Joan Ebbitt, C.S.W.-ACP has been involved in addictions treatment since 1978 with a specialty in eating disorders. She has been an innovative leader in designing treatment programs for these illnesses and has served as director and executive vice president of Clinical Programs in Dallas and Chicago. Currently in private practice, Joan has conducted numerous national education programs on eating disorders and chemical dependence. Her publications on the subject of eating illness include **The Eating Illness Workbook; Tomorrow, Monday, or New Year's Day;** and **Spinning: Thought Patterns of Compulsive Eaters.**

In her free time Joan likes to sing, walk, swim in her pool in the hot Texas summers, laugh with her friends, and sit quietly in nature, meditating on the wonders of the Universe!

Lindsey Hall

Lindsey Hall, a graduate of Stanford University, is the author of several books on eating disorders and recovery topics. Her best-known books, co-authored with Leigh Cohn, are **Bulimia: A Guide to Recovery, Self-Esteem: Tools for Recovery, Dear Kids of Alcoholics,** and **Recoveries.**

In1980, Lindsey wrote about her story in a booklet titled, **Eat Without Fear,** the first publication ever written solely about bulimia. She was the first bulimic to appear on national television, has lectured throughout the United States, has served as a member of the board of directors of Eating Disorders Awareness and Prevention (EDAP), and is editor of "The Gürze Eating Disorders Bookshelf Catalogue."

Lindsey is also an artist! She was one of the pioneers of the soft-sculpture art form, having designed and sold more than a half-million Gürze Designs dolls throughout the world in the late 1970's and early '80s. She works with her husband, Leigh Cohn, and they have two sons, Neil and Charlie.

Jane R. Hirschmann

Jane R. Hirschmann, C.S.W., is a practicing psychotherapist in New York City. She is the co-author, with Carol H. Munter, of the bestselling book, **Overcoming Overeating** and conducts Overcoming Overeating workshops with Carol throughout the United States and Europe. They are currently at work on a new book which will be published in 1994.

Jane is also the co-author of **Preventing Childhood Eating Problems** with Lela Zaphiropoulos and the co-director of the National Center for Overcoming Overeating, with headquarters in New York City and an office in Chicago.

When Jane is not busy writing, lecturing, travelling, and seeing clients, she is actively joining with others to build an anti-diet movement which will "bring the diet industry to its knees."

Marcia Germaine Hutchinson

Dr. Marcia Germaine Hutchinson is a psychologist in private practice in the Boston area, and is the author of the pioneering book, **Transforming Body Image: Learning to Love the Body You Have.** She is a Gestalt therapist noted for her creative and powerful use of therapeutic imagery. She is also an authorized practitioner of the Feldenkrais Method,™ an approach that uses movement to enhance somatic awareness.

Dr. Hutchinson is regularly invited to speak to colleagues about such diverse themes as women's issues, eating disorders, size-acceptance, therapeutic imagery, and the body-mind interface. Her book is widely used in women's centers, eating disorder clinics, and weight-loss programs throughout North America, Europe, and Australia.

She is happily married and lives in the country with her husband, Bill, and their two beloved dogs, Lina and Mr. B. She is currently working on a revised edition of her book.

Susan Kano

Susan Kano is an author and counselor who specializes in the field of weight control and eating disorders. Her ground-breaking book, **Making Peace With Food,** offers a holistic self-help program for yo-yo dieters, anorexics, and bulimics.

Susan began running workshops for chronic dieters and eating-disorder sufferers in 1980, first at Wesleyan University, next at Simmons and Wheelock Colleges in Boston, and later in private practice. Since 1991, Susan has worked toward the elimination of eating disorders and dieting on college campuses through a lecture and mini-concert called *Never Diet Again* and a seminar on eating disorder prevention for health center staff, counseling staff, athletic coaches, and resident advisors.

While a student, Susan sang in coffee houses and bars; now music is a part of her lectures and workshops. She lives in Connecticut with her husband, Jonathan Bower and their children, Eliza and Aaron.

Jane E. Latimer

Jane E. Latimer suffered from compulsive eating and bulimia for over twenty years. She is the founder and director of the Center for Emotional Eating in Denver, Colorado, and lectures and gives workshops nationally.

In addition, Jane has written and produced some unique information on recovery from addictions and on personal transformation. Her most recent work includes: **Living Binge-Free: A Personal Guide to Victory Over Compulsive Eating, The Healing Power of Inner Light-Fire: Accessing Higher Consciousness to Transform Your Life,** *Filling The Void* audio-cassette series, **Living Binge-Free Workbook/Journal,** and **Beyond the Food Game: A Spiritual & Psychological Approach to Healing Emotional Eating.**

Jane lives in Denver with her husband, Gene, and their two sons, Jesse and Cory. She looks forward to the day she can resume work on her hand-painted fabrics and quilts.

Caroline
Adams Miller

Caroline Adams Miller has been recovering from bulimia since 1984, when she first attended a free self-help group for compulsive eaters. Several years later she published her first book, **My Name is Caroline,** about her struggles with bulimia and the road to recovery. The book touched a national and international chord in many readers' minds, leading Ms. Miller to create The Foundation for Education about Eating Disorders (F.E.E.D.), which has now assisted more than 20,000 people and publishes a bi-monthly newsletter, *"Vitality!"*

Ms. Miller has also written **Feeding the Soul,** a book of meditations for compulsive eaters, and is working on her third book, **Meditations for Women Suffering from Depression,** which will be published in 1994.

Ms. Miller is married to H. Haywood Miller, III and has two children, Haywood and Samantha. They reside in Baltimore, Maryland.

Carol Munter

Carol H. Munter is a psychotherapist and certified eating disorders specialist in private practice in New York City. She started the first anti-dieting group for women in 1970. She is the co-author, with Jane R. Hirschmann, of the bestselling book, **Overcoming Overeating** and conducts Overcoming Overeating workshops with Jane throughout the United States and Europe. They are currently at work on a new book which will be published in 1994. She is also the co-director of the National Center for Overcoming Overeating, with headquarters in New York City and an office in Chicago.

Carol is excited that the 1990's feminist resurgence has brought with it "renewed attention to the oppressive nature of body hatred and dieting." She is hopeful that we will make real inroads on the problem this time around.

Judith Rabinor

Judith Ruskay Rabinor, Ph.D., is a supervisor and instructor at the Center for the Study of Anorexia and Bulimia in New York City, a consultant at Holliswood Hospital's Eating Disorder Treatment Program, and an instructor at both Greenwich Institute for Psychoanalytic Studies and at the Women's Therapy Center in New York City. Dr. Rabinor's main area of academic and clinical pursuits has focused on treatment approaches to individuals suffering from eating disorders. She has given presentations at national and international conferences, authored a number of articles, and is noted as a dynamic and interactive seminar leader.

She lives by the beach in Long Island with her two children and two cats. Her most recent interests include jewelry making and rollerblading.

Rebecca Ruggles Radcliffe

Rebecca Ruggles Radcliffe is founder and executive director of Eating Awareness Services and Education (EASE) which is dedicated to helping individuals understand eating-related issues and create healthier, fuller lives for themselves. She publishes *"The Eating Awareness and Self Enhancement Newsletter," "Developing Healthier Eating Habits," "Enlightened Eating Tape Series,"* and is the author of **Enlightened Eating: Understanding and Changing Your Relationship to Food.**

Rebecca served as vice president of The Renfrew Center prior to beginning EASE, holds a Masters degree in program development from St. Thomas College, and undergraduate degrees in communications and education from the University of Minnesota. She lectures nationally on women's issues, body image, eating disorders, and related issues.

Rebecca is currently living in Minneapolis and raising her daughter Chloe, who has taught her "the value of waking up their playful hearts."

Kim Lampson Reiff

Kim Lampson Reiff, Ph.D., author of **Eating Disorders: Nutrition Therapy in the Recovery Process,** is a psychologist in private practice in Mercer Island, Washington. She specializes in treating men and women with eating disorders, as well as survivors of sexual abuse.

Kim received her master's degree from the University of Georgia, and a doctorate in counseling psychology from the University of Washington. For several years, she authored *The Hopeline,* a newsletter for individuals concerned with eating disorders. She also serves as a board member for the Anorexia Nervosa and Bulimia Foundation and for Eating Disorders Awareness and Prevention (EDAP)–annual sponsors of Eating Disorders Awareness Week–of which she is a past-president.

Kim enjoys quilting for fun, and is devoted to her daughter, Krisanna, and her husband, Dan.

Geneen Roth

Geneen Roth is a writer and a teacher who has gained international prominence through her work in the field of eating disorders. She is the founder of *Breaking Free* workshops which she has been leading since 1979. She is the author of four best selling books: **Feeding the Hungry Heart, Breaking Free from Compulsive Eating, Why Weight?** and **When Food is Love.** She has also written for and been featured in *Time, Ms, New Woman, Family Circle,* and *Cosmopolitan.* Her poetry and short stories have been published in numerous anthologies.

Born in New York City, Geneen now lives in northern California.

Jean Rubel

Jean Bradley Rubel, Th.D. received a bachelor's degree in psychology from Occidental College in Los Angeles, California and a doctorate in theology and pastoral counseling from Berean Seminary in Wichita, Kansas. She is the founder and current president of Anorexia Nervosa and Related Eating Disorders, Inc. (ANRED), a national non-profit organization that distributes information through newsletters, booklets, workshops, and conferences.

Dr. Rubel has also coordinated a hospital eating disorders program in Oregon. She lectures across the United States and writes for various professional and general interest publications.

In her free time, Dr. Rubel enjoys gardening, hiking, and reading.

Avis Rumney

Avis Rumney is a licensed Marriage, Family, and Child Counselor in private practice in Contra Costa and Marin Counties in California. She is an eating disorders specialist and works with individuals, couples, families, and groups. Ms. Rumney herself suffered from anorexia nervosa and in the course of her treatment decided to become a therapist. She has been in private practice for ten years.

Ms. Rumney is the author of the book, **Dying to Please: Anorexia Nervosa and Its Cure,** and of the chapter, *"Soul Starvation,"* in the book **Recoveries: True Stories by People who have Conquered Addictions and Compulsions.** She is also the co-author, with Jane Rachel Kaplan and Linda Reibel, of the 1991 monograph, *"Optimal Eating: Making Personal Sense of Food and Eating."*

In addition to her work in the field of eating disorders, Ms. Rumney is an avid gardener, occasional artist, and a lover of animals and nature.

Doreen L. Virtue

Doreen L. Virtue, M.A. is a psychotherapist in private practice in Newport Beach, California. Author of **The Yo-Yo Diet Syndrome, The Chocoholic's Dream Diet,** and numerous magazine articles, she is now working on two new books, **Losing Your Pounds of Pain** for sexual abuse survivors, and **It's Up To Me: Stories of Self-Made Women.**

Doreen is the founder and director of three eating disorder units, including "The Victory Program," in southern California and "Womankind," in Nashville, Tennessee. She now specializes in treating compulsive eaters, individuals with bulimia, and survivors of sexual abuse. She gives workshops and seminars on the "Psychology of Overeating" and stress reduction techniques.

Doreen spends her leisure time attending plays at the theatre or on her rollerblades.

Order Form

Full Lives is available at bookstores and libraries. Copies may also be ordered directly from Gürze Books.

FREE Catalogue

The Gürze Eating Disorders Bookshelf Catalogue has more than 100 books, tapes, and videos on eating disorders and related topics, including many by the chapter authors of *Full Lives*. It is used as a resource by therapists, educators, and other health care professionals.

I have enclosed a check for _____ Please send me:

_____ copies of *Full Lives* — $12.95 each (1-4 copies) plus $1.95 per copy for shipping and handling

_____ copies of *Full Lives* — $10.95 each (5+ copies) plus $1.55 per copy for shipping and handling

_____ FREE copies of the *Gürze Eating Disorders Bookshelf Catalogue*

NAME _____

ADDRESS _____

CITY, ST, ZIP _____

PHONE _____

Mail a copy of this order form to:

**Gürze Books (FLV)
P.O. Box 2238
Carlsbad, CA 92018**

Phone orders accepted:
(800) 756-7533